THE EMPATHY EFFECT

The Essential Guide to Building Deeper Connections
for Success at Work and Fulfillment at Home

GRANT MORGAN

Copyright © 2025 BY Synast Publishing

Published by Synast Publishing

All rights reserved.

ISBN: 978-1-968418-09-0

INTRODUCTION

In today's fast-paced world, where digital communication often supersedes face-to-face interaction, the profound art of empathy has become more crucial than ever. This essential guide explores how empathy serves as the cornerstone for building meaningful relationships both at work and at home. It delves into the pervasive empathy gap evident in modern life—highlighting moments of disconnection that many experience, such as the misinterpretations of digital messages or the tension in workplace meetings.

Empathy is not just a buzzword; it is a transformative skill that can enhance personal and professional interactions. This book posits that empathy is vital for thriving in today's interconnected world. By acknowledging the common myths and misconceptions that surround empathy, such as the idea that it is merely about being nice or that it cannot coexist with business acumen, the book sets out to debunk these with a blend of scientific insights and real-life stories.

Readers are invited to embark on a journey of self-discovery, where they will learn to identify and overcome internal barriers to empathy, such as self-criticism and inherited biases. Through practical exercises and reflective prompts, individuals will gain the tools needed to foster deeper connections and resolve conflicts effectively. The book also addresses the challenges of maintaining empathy in digital spaces, where tone and intent can easily be misinterpreted.

What sets this guide apart is its commitment to providing actionable strategies that are rooted in scientific research and adapted for busy adults. These strategies are designed to yield immediate benefits while promoting long-term growth. By the end of this book, readers will possess a toolkit of empathy skills that can be applied daily, allowing them to cultivate fulfilling relationships and achieve greater satisfaction in all aspects of their lives.

Table of Contents

GRANT MORGAN

THE EMPATHY EFFECT

CHAPTER 1

Understanding Empathy

THE EMPATHY GAP

In this busy world, a feeling of being in lies low and gradually threads its way through the routine agendas in our day-to-day activities. Consider the dinner and the nearly lost meaning of an innocently sent email or a family dinner that goes into silence following the wrongly timed remark. Those are not isolated cases; they are indicators of a more profound problem most of us are experiencing today: the empathy gap. This gap symbolizes the distance between us and our intentions and what our interactions are in reality, and more often than not, empathy is the bridge we are missing.

The word empathy has been a misunderstood term and, in many instances, is viewed as just a formality, but empathy is a deep-rooted skill. Being empathic does not necessarily involve only being able to relate to how another person feels; rather, it involves relating with them at a level that warrants their ability to connect with that person in a way that is inexpressible using words. It is a crucial part of personal satisfaction and career excellence and affects all other areas, including our relations and psychological well-being.

The empathy held especially by individuals in an environment whose characteristics involve stress and a lot of change. At the workplace, the pressures to perform may be too dominant to note the need to have empathetic communication, creating a culture of misunderstanding and lack of attachment. In my personal life, too, the hustle and bustle of the digital connection deprives most of the subtlety of in-person connection, and it is quite simple to lose empathy.

The research shows that empathy will help to build significant and sustainable relationships and promote well-being. Research indicates that empathy has been able to enhance the dynamics within teams, enhancing job-related satisfaction and even performance. However, although empathy can be very helpful, a lot of people cannot apply it effectively. A misconception regarding the nature of empathy can cause such a struggle. It is neither about agreement nor sympathy, but it is about the desire to learn to understand the emotions of people as well as putting oneself in their place without losing oneself in the process.

The empathy gap needs to be dealt with through a deliberate attempt to build the skill of empathy. It is all about leaving the passive mode of listening and actively participating in the experiences of other people. It is about being there during a conversation, paying attention to non-verbal signals, and taking actions that seem to acknowledge how other people feel. In addition, it is the realization and the elimination of individual biases that could interfere with empathetic relationships.

Questions such as how many of these people can become a part of the journey towards healing the empathy gap also start with themselves.

Knowing how one is feeling and when the emotion is aroused is essential when it comes to building empathy towards another. This self-awareness can be cultivated by practicing mindfulness and active listening practices that may help a person stop and think before acting.

Empathy can be a means to make peace and move on in a world that seems to have lost its sense of understanding. Through their efforts to reduce the empathy gap, people may create an atmosphere of trust and comprehension at home, at work, and in their communities. The empathy gap can be a cumbersome task, but with a sense of realization and the plan to change, we can alter our relationships and, eventually, our lives.

EMPATHY AS A SKILL

Empathy as a complex competency can be looked upon as more than just purely emotional knowledge. It means being capable of sensing, knowing, and valuing the emotions of another person, which includes cognitive and emotional elements. It is not an inborn ability but a skill you become more skillful in doing with conscious effort and training, like learning a new language or playing with a musical instrument.

First, one has to learn to listen to existing empathy. This is turning inwards and trying to give attention to the person speaking so as to comprehend what exactly they are saying and their emotions and motives. Active listening is defined as eye contact and nodding, which is a sign of recognition and feedback that demonstrates understanding and interest. The process aids in building a relationship that causes the other person to feel he/she is being listened to and appreciated.

Moreover, without perspective-taking, empathy cannot be practiced, which means being able to step into the jumpsuit of another person. This is not just mental imagery of what another person is undergoing; this is having thoughts and imaginations of another person from his perspective. Such mental component of empathy helps us to see the intricacies of the situation of other people, make them closer, and understand the limitations of misunderstandings.

Another element of empathy is being aware of and controlling one's feelings. It is also important to control emotions as they enable people to remain calm and sensitive instead of being reactive. As they regulate their emotions, empathetic people can have a calming presence on others and be the support that is needed in stressful or emotionally intense scenarios.

Empathy is well entrenched in self-awareness. Knowing the limitations, the biases, and the triggering emotions will help a person empathize with other people. Such self-awareness can be assisted by self-reflection and practicing mindfulness, which will result in a more empathetic attitude towards others.

Moreover, empathy may also be developed by being exposed to other points of view. Exposing oneself to various cultures, societies, and perspectives makes one learn more about how people live and experience the world. Such exposure will overthrow stereotypes and prejudice, and this is what will shape true empathy.

Empathy is an essential technique in the workplace environment as far as leadership and teamwork are concerned. Emphatic leaders will be able to instill trust and loyalty since they are viewed as caring and thoughtful. Leaders with empathetic qualities can resolve conflicts since they know how and why the emotional processes take place, whether in the face of problems or praise. Empathic people also know how to better work with a team, as they can work with different personalities and promote an inclusive atmosphere where all people feel important.

However, empathy has to be moderated with boundaries that can avoid burnout. Excesses of empathy may result in burnout emotions. Hence, it is imperative to have boundaries and self-care in order to remain in good condition despite the ability to empathize.

To summarize the picture, empathy as a skill is a combination of listening and understanding mixed with emotion management. It is something that has to be practiced on an ongoing basis and requires a contribution to build and support. By developing empathy, one is able to improve personal and professional relationships and lead to a world where people are more connected and understanding.

TYPES OF EMPATHY

Empathy, being a multifactorial and deep-rooted facet of human interaction, may be divided into three types, namely cognitive, emotional, and compassionate empathy. These two types have different characteristics in the forms in which people can feel and respond to the emotions and experiences of other people and develop a deep and meaningful relationships with them.

A common misinterpretation is the so-called view of perspective, also known as cognitive empathy, i.e., cognitively transcending the mind with important thoughts and emotions into the mind of the other without having to share their emotional experience. This form of empathy is essential when there is a need to know what a reason causes a person or what they feel, and it is mostly applied in instances of negotiation or when resolving a conflict. To give an example, a manager may engage in cognitive empathy to understand the reason why an employee is frustrated with a new policy, thus being able to effectively address concerns without necessarily being frustrated himself or herself.

The other type is emotional empathy, which consists of being able to experience the feelings that an individual is demonstrating literally. This type of empathy is usually in the realm of the gut, such that a greater sense of contact exists on an emotional level. It is that which makes people weep when a friend is raped or rejoices when a loved one is winning. Emotional empathy comes in very handy, especially when there is a need for seriousness and understanding, as is the case when talking to a friend about loss. However, it can also result in empathy fatigue when properly controlled because it can be quite taxing always to assume the feelings of other people.

Compassionate empathy or empathic concern takes this further so that not only does a person recognize and experience the emotions of another, but a person is also driven to respond to them. It is the sort of empathy that makes one bring food to the neighbor who lost a loved one or help out a suffering colleague. When the knowledge of cognitive empathy and the emotional relationship of emotional empathy are joined with the proactive aspect, then this form of empathy becomes particularly effective in creating positive societies and relationships.

There are advantages and possible risks in each category of empathy. Although cognitive empathy plays an important role in regard to understanding and communication, it may often be viewed as being cold or detached when not complemented with emotional or compassionate empathy. Though emotional empathy is crucial to building strong personal relationships, it can also result in burnout when a person pays too much attention to the emotional experiences of other people. Although compassionate empathy stimulates a person to act, it should be considered carefully to prevent crossing the line and taking responsibility for another person's well-being.

Being aware of the existence of these various kinds of empathy enables a person to have a better understanding of how to approach their relationships with other people and adjust their approach to empathy based on the needs of each given scenario. Identification of individual empathy strengths and weaknesses allows for the achievement of a more harmonious and efficient empathetic perspective and, therefore, a more harmonious way of dealing with people, both on a personal and working level. Moreover, the establishment of empathy in its different forms may result in stronger community persons being more prepared to assist each other in hardships, which will eventually become a culture of communicating and treating one another with respect and understanding.

EMPATHY MYTHS DEBUNKED

When it comes to the sphere of empathy, the myths go along, and most of the time, they blur the real power and the potential of empathy. This is a major misunderstanding that many people have when it comes to empathy. They think of empathy as a soft skill activity, and that is a lot of those who are too sensitive. But, the myths water down the strong positive effects and the versatility of empathy, particularly in leadership and self-development.

The first popular myth is that empathy is agreeing with people all the time. Nevertheless, empathy is not that which is felt when agreements are made but when there is understanding. It means listening attentively to someone's point of view without necessarily agreeing with them. This is an important differentiation, particularly in the field of conflict resolution, where empathy may overcome the differences without risking the loss of personal and organizational values. As an example, an empathetic leader could agree with one of the employees that changing the deadline is a frustrating experience without giving in to unrealistic requests.

One more myth is that empathy is something inborn, a gift that only some can be lucky to have. It is also true that empathy is not a skill that can be practiced and developed through an act of mindfulness. Studies indicate that empathy is not a skill that is unattainable by some people; it can actually develop over time and through certain activities and meditation.

The concept of empathy is highly misconstrued with the likes of sympathy and enabling, which may result in adverse consequences. Sympathy is the ability to pity oneself, and this may give a distance. Enabling can do the same with the pretense of helping since negative acts may be encouraged. Empathy, in turn, is somewhere in the middle ground; it involves being there, being able to understand, not falling into the emotions of another person, and not letting the dangerous dynamics flourish.

Skewed perceptions of empathy have also been enhanced by the media and, more importantly, popular psychology. The phrase toxic positivity, along with simplistic directives and narratives like listen more, cannot represent how empathy is complex. These impressions may cause a reductionist view of empathetic exposure, which is shallow and ineffective.

It is imperative to familiarize ourselves with myths about empathy so that we can fully utilize it. Knowing how to clear these misconceptions, individuals, and organizations can adjust their expectations and view empathy as a tool of connection and communication. It is not an abstract reset but an actual one that represents a scientific alternative to the pop psychology that tends to make empathy sound insignificant.

In addition, empathy entails not only emotional connections but cognitive ones as well. It incorporates the capacity to predict what another person is feeling based on their point of view, emotional empathy, which relates to how a person feels, and compassionate empathy, which is action-driven. There are different types of benefits for each of them: business negotiations and emotional assistance in personal interaction.

With the established concept of empathy as an identifiable, transformable skill, people can work on their relationships much more smoothly, creating a world in which empathy can be taken to positive knowledge and cooperation. At work or home, breaking these myths enables individuals to exercise empathy smartly, improve their relationships, and make society more empathetic.

CHAPTER 2

The Science Behind Empathy

NEUROSCIENCE OF EMPATHY

Kindheartedness, which is a key component of social connection in human beings, happens to be a fantasizing grouping that is closely associated with the plan of the cerebrum and its activities. The most important thing to know in learning the neuroscience of empathy is that of the kind of neurons called mirror neurons, which are stimulated when we act ourselves and when we are looking at another person who is acting in the same manner. The process of mirroring offers a brain basis to our empathic process, so people can understand other people faster and on a subconscious level by imagining how the other person feels and what the other person is doing.

These neurons mostly dwell in the premotor cortex and the inferior parietal lobule, which are the regions of the brain concerned with generating and performing movements. When we watch a person smile, our mirror neurons assume the stance of smiling, and we experience very much the same emotions, which makes them share. Such neural mirroring draws the biological roots of empathy, which allows us to experience what the other one experiences, to some degree, and allows embedding and achieving social connectivity and comprehension.

Mirror neurons are, however, not the only prerequisite to empathy. It also involves the emotional and cognitive circuits of the brain, insula, and anterior cingulate cortex, which process and control emotions. The insula assists us in the visceral answers associated with emotions, including the frostiness of fear or the heat of happiness. In the meantime, the anterior cingulate cortex helps us purpose and manage our feelings, which is vital in the differentiation between self and others and, therefore, enables us to achieve empathy without losing touch with who we are.

The empathic neural circuitry is complicated and depends on numerous variables such as genetics, surroundings, and experiences. Hereditary tendencies may influence the density and effectiveness of mirror neurons, whereas the environment, such as a childhood or cultural set-up, influences the manifestation and perception of empathy. As an example, a person who is brought up in a supportive community might develop more empathetic reactions than others who have a damaging background.

In addition to this, neurochemicals like oxytocin and dopamine also regulate empathy to augment social connections and encourage the reward of empathy-related behaviors. Also known as the love hormone, oxytocin allows people to trust and form attachments, and they are more open to the feelings of others. Dopamine, which is a part of the brain reward system, enhances empathetic behaviors by giving the feeling of pleasure and contentment when bonding with others.

Although it is very important, empathy may not be the same in every person because of neurodiversity. Mental conditions like autism spectrum disorder, among others, may influence the processing of empathy, and alternative techniques of social engagement and emotional resonance may be necessary. In the same way, empathetic responses may be variously impacted by cultural differences, which is why empathy is likely to be a learned behavior.

To conclude, the neuroscience of empathy shows that it is a complex construct that has a network of neural and chemical interactions. Knowledge of these underlying mechanisms not only helps in understanding how empathy works but also paves the way to achieving a more empathetic society due to the ability to improve empathy in a specific manner due to techniques and education.

MIRROR NEURONS IN ACTION

When it comes to neuroscience, mirror neurons are an interesting phenomenon that narrows the distance between comprehending and feeling the emotions of other human beings. These neurons, which are mostly found within the premotor cortex and also within the inferior parietal lobule, trigger not only when one completes a task but also when one watches another person doing the same. The mechanism of mirroring is a neurological explanation of empathy, showing that it is possible to share the emotions and even senses of others just by observing them.

Now, imagine that you observe an individual hitting his thumb with a hammer. When you view someone who seems to be experiencing pain, you may unconsciously flinch or grimace as though you were experiencing the pain. The reaction here is not just a trained reaction but an indication of the mirror neuron system doing its action. These neurons help us know and feel what others are doing and feeling, and it becomes a critical side of social cognition and communication.

Mirror neurons not only help in physical actions but are also useful in emotional resonance. Our mirror neurons activate when we witness a person smiling, which leads to the same emotional response in us. This is how emotions are mirrored; easy connection and understanding are possible, and we are able to share solidarity in the emotions of joy, sadness, or pain that others are going through, which is what makes human interaction so colorful.

We observe the impact of the mirror neurons in different cases of everyday life. Think of a manager whose mood does not very visibly to the rest of the team. A happy attitude may inspire and support, whereas a gloomy spirit may dim the particular mood. This reflects the fact that emotions are contagious, making leaders responsible for ensuring that their expressions of emotions are controlled. The ripple effect that a single person's mood has on a group dynamic demonstrates the huge social influence that the mirror neurons have.

Nevertheless, the knowledge about mirror neurons is an issue that should be studied with some reserve. Although they give information regarding how empathy works, they are not the only explanation of this intricate human characteristic. Empathy is complex and requires a mixture of both emotional and cognitive empathy; it entails cognitive processes more than a simple mirroring, according to which one takes the standpoint of another; that is, one empathizes-identifies. In that way, mirror neurons provide a foundation for empathetic relationships, but they belong to a bigger system that can help us engage with other people in meaningful ways.

Moreover, the fact that people have different responses to emotional appeal indicates that the functioning of the mirror neurons differs among individuals. Neurodiversity and cultural disparities are some of the factors that can affect the manner in which the brain reacts to people's emotional states. To provide an example, people with autism spectrum behavior can also have altered patterns of activation of mirror neurons, which impacts their levels of empathetic responses. Endomorphic cultural norms, in a similar fashion, influence the externalities with regard to expressing emotions and perceiving them, further complicating the influence of the mirror neuron.

As it turns out as concluding remarks, although mirror neurons play a crucial role in learning the biological basis of empathy, they are only a part of the solution. Their revelation has shed light on the field of neuroscience, offering valuable resources for the human ability to relate with others and be empathetic. As further research is carried out, it will be an exciting prospect that this knowledge can be utilized to improve interpersonal relationships and even learn to be more empathetic.

EMPATHY AND EVOLUTION

Empathy is one of the central threads of human evolution and the overall fabric of human interaction and cooperation in the complex tapestry of it. Early humans, in the pursuit of survival in the large and sometimes dangerous landscape of the land, found that it was easier to achieve this when working together. Empathy in this context was not only a moral compass but something of evolutionary benefits. It contributed to the development of close teams, in which it became necessary to interpret and react to the moods of other people, signs of which should have been perceived in the surrounding environment.

Biological origins of empathy can be traced to the development of interpersonal neurons, a very interesting feature of our neural wiring whereby we can feel what others feel and do what they do as we do it. It is not a peculiarity of how our brain is wired but a really remarkable part of how we learn to connect. It allows us to sympathize with the pain of a friend, rejoice over the victory of a colleague, or even twitch over the loss of a stranger. It is through such common experiences that the social connections through which human society has focused and progressed have evolved.

More than staying alive, empathy has driven culture and civilization. It is a foundation of moral thoughts and ethics based on which human actions are discussed. The ability to empathize and feel the emotions of another person has resulted in the establishment of laws, norms, and practices that facilitate fairness and justice. The truth is simply that empathy is the non-verbal builder of the communities that put social welfare before personal profitability.

Emotional connectedness expands into empathy areas in interspecies interactions in the case of human beings. The relationships of humans and animals are also evidence of the broad power of empathy. An animal domestication process, as an example, is a hapless history of shared knowledge and sympathy. The relationship with animals has resulted in the domestication process that was vital in agricultural development and company through humankind engaging with animals with the aim of understanding.

Nevertheless, the history of empathy does not go without complications. With the increase in size and diversity of societies, barriers to empathy have only proliferated. Empathy gaps the gap between civilizations is the inability to understand the other party because of the hustle and bustle of everyday life and the influence of technology and the internet. The digital age is one in which we may feel connected with each other in quite unprecedented manners. Yet, it speaks of a paradox in which the superficial interactions may tend to mimic the meaningful ones.

When it comes to handling such issues, it is of pivotal importance to note that empathy is a skill that can be enhanced and developed. As past ancestors developed their instincts of empathy to survive, human beings today should affirmatively develop this ability to adapt to the contemporary world of interdependence. One of the practices that can help to eliminate the empathy gap would be active listening, mindfulness, and reflective conversation, which can help to develop stronger connections between people despite the various divergent cultures and communities.

Empathy, consequently, is not something that is amid our evolutionary history but something in action that still defines our future. It is the pump of human life, which unifies various beats into a beautiful story of life togetherness. In the face of the modern world and its challenges, empathy serves as a doorway not only to the realization of oneself but also to the future in which people are better-spirited and united.

EMPATHY IN PSYCHOLOGY

Empathy is a bridge in the complex world of human emotions that places the interrelationship between two or more people at many levels. The psychology profession analyzes empathy on a micro-level, identifying the key elements of the term, which gives a complex picture of how it can be used to bring humans together. In this journey, we will examine the cognitive, emotional, and compassionate aspects of empathy and what role they play in helping us know and be moved by the feelings of others.

Perspective-taking, which is frequently explained as cognitive empathy, allows people to have an understanding of the thoughts and emotions another person experiences. It is the mental intuition of what one may be going through, as a manager tells when he/she realizes that an employee is frustrated due to failing to meet the deadline. Such empathy is especially useful during the negotiation and conflict resolution process when a better knowledge of the other side of a case can precondition more effective communication and finding solutions. Nevertheless, cognitive empathy cannot always be as deep as a person need in order to connect with someone because it operates on the rational mind.

Emotional empathy is beyond intellectual and enables people to identify with the feelings of others in an emotional state. The components of such empathy may be seen in something as straightforward as a person crying with a friend after the loss of their pet, as this is experiencing another person emotionally. Emotional empathy exists in crises and offers hot feelings and welcoming support, which words can never demonstrate. However, it poses a danger of emotional contagion when a person can be affected by someone in distress. In that regard, there should be emotional boundaries that help one sustain emotional health.

Compassionate empathy, or empathic concern, combines the insight of cognitive empathy with the experiential power of emotional empathy, driving one to perform active support. It is the motive force behind doing good things, and this could be in the form of sharing food with a mourning neighbor or simply helping out a distressed associate. This is not just empathy that identifies the feelings of other people but further pushes one to ease their pain, thus promoting the spirit of altruism and social duty.

The interaction between these forms of empathy has highly complicated neuro processes. As an example, mirror neurons are critical in involuntary matching and interpretation of the emotion of the other. This is a neurological basis that justifies the fact of contagion of yawns or cringing when one sees another person suffer. But, although mirror neurons give us a biological explanation of the process of empathy, they by no means put the whole picture of empathy and do not explain all the manifestations of empathy because the process of empathy is highly contingent and depends on personal lifetimes, cultural backgrounds and personal experiences among others.

Empathy is considered to be a living skill in psychological practice as opposed to a trait. It can be developed and improved deliberately via constructive practice and thought. By urging people to participate in the development of empathy exercises, e.g., role-play or mindfulness, one can enable them to develop more emotional intelligence and effectiveness in their interactions. These can improve not only personal relationships but also the more wholesome organizational cultures and benevolent societies.

In conclusion, empathy as a psychological phenomenon is a complex phenomenon that enhances human interaction by promoting understanding, compassion, and contact. It enables human beings to rise above individual prejudice and connect to the experiences of other individuals genuinely. The more we can delve into the levels of empathy, the more power it holds to change the personal front and even the social front significantly, and this can be utilized to make the world a kinder and more emotional place.

CHAPTER 3

Building Self-Empathy

SELF-COMPASSION PRACTICES

When it comes to fostering empathy, self-compassion turns out to be a significant practice, as its foundation is the building block of viable emotional relations with other people. This practice starts by knowing that no one can actually extend real empathy to others without first having compassion towards oneself. It is just like the saying that one should have his oxygen mask on and then be able to help others.

Self-compassion consists of being able to identify with our fellow humans, as we are all imperfect, and independently of how unkind we are to one another, being able to forgive ourselves as we would another friend. It is not a self-indulgence, it is not a lowering of standards, but it is a job of creating an internal environment in which personal development and resiliency can flourish. It has been discovered that self-compassion mitigates anxiety and depression and adopts a healthier state of mind, which is more helpful in spreading empathy to others.

Another basic point about self-compassion is the possibility of being in touch with our thoughts and emotions without judging them: a mindful state. This non-judgment awareness assists us in seeing our experiences in their ratio rather than exaggerating them with an unjust judgment against self. Mindfulness self-compassion tries to make us moderate our negative feelings in such a manner that we are able to think about them and not get affected by them.

In order to bring about self-compassion, there are a number of practices that can be implemented to help an individual have a more friendly relationship with themselves. One of the easiest but most effective exercises is the self-compassion break, which is when one recognizes when he or she is suffering and reminds oneself that other humans struggle with the same issues, and then speaks kind words to oneself. Minding one of such practices, people would be able to reform their inner monologues, discarding the role of cruel self-judgment and embracing support and compassion.

The other effective approach is taking guided self-talk scripts when one fails or when one feels very disappointed. These scripts assist in recontextualizing negative thoughts and encourage more caring internal self-talk. As an example, rather than thinking about their inadequacies, they could reason with themselves and say, I am doing the best I can, and that is good enough. The affirmations boost the feeling of self-esteem and increase emotional strength.

Moreover, it is important to include mindfulness techniques, such as short daily practices, that help to foster self-compassion to a considerable extent. Making mindful breathing or using the three breaths technique would give a brief moment of detaching and reconnecting with oneself and induce feelings of peace and focus. The practices are especially useful in environments characterized by high levels of stress since it is in this type of environment that people are more inclined toward negative self-talk.

The other beneficial element in the self-compassion toolbox is journaling. Continuous contemplation of experience allows one to specifically observe trends in self-harshness and actively change a mental attitude towards a more humane one. Some journaling questions are like: What did I learn today? or What am I thankful for? It can also direct this reflective process, which amplifies positive self-awareness and development.

Finally, being self-compassionate is all about establishing a belief in self-respect and kindness. It teaches people that they are capable of flowing through life and different circumstances with an understanding heart and compassion not only for other people but also for themselves. When we develop self-compassion, we develop a supportive environment inside ourselves, where we may develop empathy, which may spill out into our interactions and relations and enhance them. This personal revolution is the secret of creating a more understanding and bonded world.

OVERCOMING SELF-CRITICISM

The internal dialogue can be called the roadmap in the complicated territory of personal civilization, as well as the obstacle. Such a dialogue, especially when filled with self-criticism, may prove to be a tremendous barrier to empathy, at least to oneself but also others. This process of recovery is traveling through a journey of replacing this inner voice with one that builds and not one that undermines it.

Self-criticism does not only exist as an internal monologue; it is, in fact, a deep impact that determines the further interaction with the world. It usually takes a forceful, merciless tone that criticizes all the wrong moves and blows out of proportion the shortcomings. This is an internalized voice that may hamper the way we relate to others and understand them because the emotion level depleted by this voice gets deprived of the required empathic resources. Such negativity does not only have an internal effect, but it also spills out of us and has an effect on our relationships and even on the quality of our relationships.

The initial opportunity to overcome self-criticism is to know that it exists and realize its causes. Self-criticism, which is usually based on experiences or expectations of society or beliefs that an individual holds or assumes, also survives best in places where perfection is a prerequisite. These origins are not only important to define but also to be able to see this voice through a more humane point of view about why this voice exists and what possible purpose it has served at one point in time.

The change of self-criticism is possible when one practices with the goal of learning to be compassionate toward oneself. One of the areas where they are effective is cognitive behavioral therapy (CBT) techniques, which involve prescribed procedures for reframing negative thoughts. The process of validating self-critical ideas and substituting these affirmations with balanced and realistic ones helps people change their inner stories. The other potent tool that can be used is the writing of kind letters to oneself as though a good friend is being addressed. The activity not only fosters kindness but also teaches empathy towards oneself and one's hardships and flaws.

Mindfulness also helps in getting rid of self-criticism. Mindfulness promotes an open and non-judgmental attitude to oneself and one's thoughts and feelings, enabling a person to keep them within sight without being caught up in them. Examples of techniques that may facilitate the development of an attitude of being present in the moment and an attitude of acceptance include mindful breathing or body scans, which may reduce the strength of self-critical thoughts.

Testimony of the changed self-statements demonstrates a significant effect of such practices. Those who have adopted self-compassion acknowledge not only the feeling of increased self-esteem but also building stronger relationships and being able to look at other people and be empathetic towards them. These accounts are testimonies of how powerful a change from self-judgment to self-encouragement is.

In conclusion, combating self-criticism does not involve turning off the voice of the inner critic but changing him/her into a positive mentor. Once cultivating a nurturing and supportive internal conversation, a person will open their way to empathy with themselves, as well as others. Such transformation is an essential measure of creating an empathic foundation that is strong and lasting, leading to the realization of deeper and more meaningful relationships in all spheres of life.

RECOGNIZING PERSONAL BIASES

Biases are like the invisible partners of our human interaction dance, subliminally telling us what to do and how and who to think about. These prejudices embedded deep into our unconscious mind influence our cognition about the things around us and other people. It is essential to identify such personal biases to develop a true sense of empathy and connection.

Bias is not an evil superimposed on our minds; it is an association line, preconceived, due to our minds through lifelong experience in order to make a bit of everyday life easier in a complicated world. Left on their own, nevertheless, they might overcome our judgment and block empathy in its true sense. These biases also come in many different forms and include the more flagrant likes, racial or gender bias, and the more subtle, such as affinity biases, where we develop a preference for those who are similar to ourselves.

Personal bias is one of the most dangerous factors because it is not easy to detect. As compared to overt prejudices, biases are the personal kind, and as opposed to the latter, these prejudices work implicitly in the shadows of our conscious attention. As an example, an employee may attract the attention of a manager subconsciously, and the contributions made by employees with a similar background or interest may be deemed more positively by the manager than the contributions made by other employees. These biases may cause groups of people to think and act in a similar way, which supposes creativity and innovation.

In starting the process of identification and response to these biases, self-understanding is important. This is a conscious and continuous habit of self-introspection and seeking critical evaluations. Such tests as the Implicit Association Test (IAT) can help us understand our unconscious likes and aversions. Also, it can be helpful to keep a so-called bias journal in which a person notes down when they have made snap judgments and assumptions. These practices allow people to openly stand up against their prejudices, turning the previously existing invisible walls into a chance for improvement and learning.

There are numerous stories about how the awareness and active fulfillment of identification and reactions to prejudice can radically transform a personality. As an illustration, one can talk about the case of a teacher who did not realize how culturally biased she was in her understanding of the situation with the behavior of a student who was not interested in the subject of a lesson. She was shocked by this realization, and this experience led to a more inclusive and empathetic classroom culture. These stories highlight the strength of self-discovery, empathy, and connection.

A culture that promotes inclusion and diversity cannot be achieved with simple soul-searching; rather, it should be implemented on an organizational level. Suggestions and open discussions in groups and communities can unveil the invisible prejudices and create a more inclusive setting. The most effective and best way of facilitating continuity of awareness and change is a peer feedback circle where people report their observations on one another in a non-threatening environment with regard to biases.

Besides, structural changes can be carried out by the organization to counter the impacts of the biases. This consists of diversification of hiring panels, conducting frequent unconscious bias training, and providing clear policies that encourage equality and inclusivity. These practices can be systematically incorporated into the culture of an organization. In such a way, the biases can be eliminated, leading to a more understanding and emotionally close work environment.

In conclusion, it is crucial to understand that being aware of personal biases is not a place but a process; rather, it is the same game of trying to divide great theories of the world. It involves being humble, being vulnerable, and being bold enough to make changes. By so doing, we are not just increasing our ability to empathize. Still, we are also enriching our experiences in our relations with people around us, having a more organic and more sincere attachment to them.

SETTING PERSONAL BOUNDARIES

Defining personal boundaries in empathy is not just essential to create some barrier and defend oneself, but it is a major step in self-care and healthy treatment of others. It is a skill that needs to deal with the narrow border between being safe and keeping open-handed relationships. When implemented, boundaries can be a guide to genuine interactions with empathy growing unhindered.

Boundaries are what they are all about; this is because it helps to distinguish between empathic involvement and self-preservation. They are like the invisible boundary line demarcating the beginning and the end of the personal space, and they preserve emotional energy, as well as promote good relationships. Boundaries do not divide as walls do; instead, they enable the inward passage of empathy but not emotional depletion and anger.

Take the case of a therapist who restricts the days of the visit, say to a few sessions a day. This boundary does not mean any empathy, but it is a promise to stand by the quality-of-service delivery to the clients. Conservation of her own mental and emotional faculties would enable the therapist to be present enough and effective at every session. The rule is general in the case of work, family, and friends.

To establish limits, one will need to be both clear and compassionately firm. It starts with acknowledging boundaries and giving a premium to one's needs as much as other peoples. Language is actually a deciding factor here, a medium between intent and meaning. Statements such as, I would like to assist. Still, I am in the middle of something first before I can serve you at your full potential, or I love you, and I also require some tranquility in order to recharge and show the value of a need of both parties.

The difficulty is usually in dispelling the guilt that comes with putting boundaries. Some are afraid of being rejected or disappointed, or they are afraid they will be viewed as selfish. The surrender to the importance of boundaries, however, ultimately brings more trust and respect. When a manager refuses to accept other responsibilities to concentrate on the current ones, this will establish a precedence that rewards quality over quantity, which, in the end, is to the advantage of the team.

Real-life vignettes show how boundaries can change relationships. A teacher who had set up firm boundaries in his classroom found that students reacted with greater respect and investment in what occurred. In the same way, friendship can be reinforced on the basis of truthful discussions concerning individual boundaries, which results in respect and empathy.

In addition, the practice of establishing boundaries cannot be discussed without a reference to empathy fatigue acknowledgment and mitigation. This state of affairs, which is characterized by fatigue and loss of touch, is usually a result of an overabundance of emotional focus. Irritability and apathy are only some of the early warning signs that people can learn to prevent.

Self-assessment tools and reflection skills will help them maintain boundaries. A single walk after a hard day or a silence after a tiring talk and the like will be a good reset ritual. Such practices not only maintain the status of emotional health but also improve the ability to invest empathetically.

Finally, by establishing personal boundaries, we do not exclude others but rather invite people to continue and strengthen the relationship. Inconsiderable boundary setting helps anyone maintain his or her integrity and, at the same time, creates an atmosphere where people can be empathetic. Such a balance is necessary for real and lasting relationships, and empathy can be a sustainable enhancement in our lives.

CHAPTER 4

Empathy in Relationships

EMPATHY IN FAMILY LIFE

Empathy is one of the foundations of the complex family tapestry, and it can support the understanding and connection between the members. At home, empathy is not a passive sentient activity but an experience that needs consideration, patience, and hard work. It is the capability of being sensitive to the feelings of the members of the family and connecting to them so that you form a friendly atmosphere in which members of the family are appreciated and their feelings are understood.

The most important part of empathy development within families is active listening. It is not enough to merely listen to the words that are uttered; one has to be more in tune with the emotional undertones and unspoken messages that tend to go with the spoken word. An example of such behavior can also be demonstrated by the parents, especially in terms of giving their children maximum attention, making eye contact, and providing supporting gestures and words to their offspring. These interactions restore the confidence of a child and make him or her talk more so that he can be heard.

Family life thrives on experience and rituals of empathy, which enforce bonding. Rituals, such as weekly dinners, game nights, and bedtime stories, are family occasions in which empathy can thrive. With such rituals, a family member gets a structured place to discuss their ups and downs, and a culture of freedom and support develops in the family. In these activities, the members of the family learn to share the happiness of others and give them the necessary comfort in difficult situations.

Besides, empathy demands the capacity to view from the point of view of another individual. It is so important in the case of siblings, where sometimes it is easy to feel the rivalry and lack of understanding. However, role-play activities and parent-child discussions will enable instructors to teach children to literally walk in the other person's shoes by instructing them to explain how they believe the brother/sister will feel in a certain circumstance. The practice not only helps them to improve their empathy levels but also reinforces their conflict-resolution abilities.

Parents are the key to developing an empathic family setting. They can achieve this by being an example to their children and others on how to be or show empathy. Being empathetic means not ignoring the feelings of the individuals in the family, not judging their experiences, but reacting in a caring way. As an example, when a child says he or she is angry, a parent would respond by saying, I see that you are angry. Instead of rejecting their feelings, talk to them about what is bothersome to them. Other than providing a solution to the instant emotional need, the method is also a learning process for the child on how to manage his/her emotions healthily.

Also, family conflicts should be resolved in an understanding manner to help convert conflicts into instances of learning and self-development. Families should not regard individual conflicts as negative experiences but as an opportunity to find out more about what other members are thinking and what their needs are. Such attitude adjustment can provide more successful interactions and better relations.

Honestly, empathy in a family is simply providing a home where every member can become visible, audible, and appreciated. It is all about establishing a base of trust and respect where emotions are accepted, and differences are to be celebrated. Families can set up an emotionally healthy environment by incorporating empathy into the thread of everyday communication and family customs, with these measures helping to prepare the individuals within a family unit to strengthen emotionally and socially and thrive. Besides contributing to family life, this is the setting that prepares people to survive in the wider society with empathy needs.

EMPATHY IN ROMANTIC RELATIONSHIPS

Empathy turns out to be one of the keys to the dance of romantic relationships, and couples should be taught to keep it well. This is a skill crafted emotion-wise that many may easily confuse or refer to as simple sympathy, but this requires you to know and understand each other regarding the strains you feel and the insights you hold. The process of empathy in the relationship of two people who are in love is not only about exposure to the emotions of the other party but also about the possibility of the ability to maintain space to allow the other to be in that emotional state without the need to resolve or criticize.

It is important to notice the distinction between sympathy and empathy. Sympathy may entail pitying a partner, and empathy may entail putting oneself in the position of a partner and sharing the world of emotions with a partner. It has to be about slowing down and listening and not about just running in to provide fixes and offers. This difference is especially important in conflicts or emotional events. In this case, empathy serves as a mediator since it links partners when conflicts occur.

The most important skill in the practice of empathy in relationships is holding the space. The idea here is to be wholly present in the emotions of a partner and enable them to express themselves without interruption and judgment. It is the art of attempting to resist the temptation to fill voids with words of advice or timidity and being there but in silence. The latter may be difficult, as it involves being vulnerable, able to tolerate uncertainty, and dealing with both personal and the partner thereof.

Communication is indeed paramount in cultivating empathy. The open-ended questions and listening to the responses are effective in assisting the partners to know what is in their minds and feelings. Expressions such as, help me know what you are going through or, what can I do for you now? I will be able to open the doors to more profound knowledge and feeling. These questions teach partners to communicate their emotions and needs, develop an attitude to solve problems, and support each other.

Empathy also consists of understanding boundaries and respecting them. It has to be noted that there is no need to lose oneself in the feelings of others and to share their problems through empathy. Boundaries enable a couple to experience their distinctiveness and emotional well-being, which is necessary to last a long time. For empathy, there must be the right amount of togetherness and separation so that partners are accessible to each other emotionally, but also by giving each other space and allowing them to do what they please.

Further, in relation to romantic relationships, empathy implies a promise of eternal evolvement and change. Partners change with time, and so do their emotional needs and the manner of expressing them. It is this ability to skillfully engage in repeat discussion that makes a specific part of this dynamic relationship, where there is a consistent attempt to get to know and be compassionate with the varying terrains of one another. Routine appointments with each other (daily appointments or even weekly appointments) will be of great help to keep the partners on the same track and sensitive to what the partner is in a particular state of mind and heart.

Lastly, empathy is an element that provides a shield against some of the drawbacks of relationships, which include miscommunication and resentment. This is achieved by developing a culture of empathy among partners so that they achieve a successful relationship that fulfills the emotional needs of individuals and is healthy. Empathy, in turn, is a life-changer of romantic relationships as the aspect that awaited conflict becomes an avenue of closer ties and understanding of each other.

PARENTING WITH EMPATHY

As a parent, the spirit of empathy is one of the pillars that many are encouraged to use in raising emotionally resilient and smart children. The process of being a caring parent starts when we literally put ourselves in the place of the young ones and come to perceive their world no longer as adults in miniature but as individuals with their special views and worlds. The process involves active listening on the part of parents and responding with validation, where parents cannot use solutions right away or dismiss the emotions of their children.

The core of empathetic parenting is being able to be a role model when it comes to emotional intelligence. The best learning style for children is through emulating the adults in the environment. Sharing their feelings with the parent, a child learns the expression of feelings and, at the same time, normalizes their own emotions, which is an extremely valuable lesson, especially when handled by stating that a parent is feeling frustrated at the moment but is taking a deep breath. Such openness creates a situation when a person would not feel frightened of their feelings but rather comprehend and handle them positively.

What is important in this practice is to adjust the communication strategies depending on the stages at which children are in. In the case of toddlers, the process of emotion naming would give them a chance to identify and name their feelings. A parent may also tell a child when he/she is upset, and the child may say that he/she is upset because he/she cannot find his/her toy, and this aids the child in relating words to emotion. To school-aged kids and teenagers, conversations may be able to shift to talk about more complex issues, whether it is traversing peer relationships or getting to grips with tricky news stories, always using open-ended questions to steer the talk.

Parenting empathy is also through the establishment of rituals that support connection and understanding. Building on family empathy can strengthen family relationships; family empathy rituals can include a weekly empathy circle after dinner, where every family member relates one high and one low of his/her week. These kinds of practices also establish an open platform where people can express themselves and receive support, which establishes a culture of sympathy that stretches beyond certain members of a particular family.

Another essential element is the Emphatic Navigation of Conflicts. Conventional approaches to conflict resolution usually focus on instant apologies, which is not a guarantee of understanding and resolution. The parents can instead give exercises such as Switch Shoes, where the siblings can define a situation in the voice of the other. This also relieves aggression and creates a habit of taking others' views and respect.

Empathy can be quite an effective instrument even during situations of considerable tension, like meltdowns. Knowing about the "downstairs brain" or the limbic system helps parents realize why logic does not work during emotional storms. Empathy scripts, i.e., You are now furious. I am here with you," assure the kid that his/her feelings are normal and reassure him/her by just being there present, without running to solve the issue.

Parenting with empathy, in the final analysis, is more about creating a situation where children feel noticed, listened to, and appreciated. It is to show them that the way they feel is real and that they are able to cope with it and have all they need to do so. This empathetic base not only makes the contact between parents and children more durable but also helps children acquire the emotional qualities that the children will need to meet the world around them empathically and boldly.

MANAGING CONFLICT WITH EMPATHY

Conflict is like trying to ride a whirlpool, and it takes a very delicate balance of knowledge and emotional awareness. This is because conflict management with empathy is all about acknowledging that each disagreement is a potential springboard toward greater understanding instead of being a scene where one should ask who is right. It is putting oneself in the position of another one, attempting to build a viewpoint about the situation, and not coming up with premature conclusions and solutions.

Empathy when handling a conflict involves listening, and this goes beyond hearing the sounds that people say. It will demand focus on the feelings and the motives of those words. This is laying aside one's judgments and prejudices and listening and being really concerned with what the other is saying. Active listening implies nodding in recognition, eye contact, and exclamatory forms of encouragement such as I see or that must be hard on you. These actions do not only confirm the emotion of the speaker but also precondition a clearer and open talk.

During war fighting, people may lose control and develop heightened emotions that may create a hostile standoff. Empathy, in this case, is a reassuring agent. One can defuse it by appealing to the emotion involved, whether it is frustration, disappointment, or anger. As an illustration of this, saying things like, I know you are angry about this, will help to put on record how the other party feels, which in most cases will calm them down and open up avenues of reconciliation.

The other important features of empathetic conflict management include the act of asking open-ended questions. Questions like: Can you assist me in comprehending the significance of this matter to you? What can we, as part of it, do to deal with this situation? Encourage mutual problem-solving instead of opposition discussion. The given strategy not only facilitates the collection of additional information but also indicates readiness to collaborate to reach a win-win solution.

Moreover, empathy presupposes the necessity to stay composed and able to control one's emotional state. This entails being aware of when personal biases or stressors may be causing the interaction and putting a pause in order to reset. Deep breathing, counting to ten, or resting even during a conversation can work as a method of keeping fit as long as the person is not crying.

The force of empathy in conflict is that it converts the oppositional relationships to understanding and growth. There is more possibility of the two parties overcoming their differences and striking a point of agreement when they feel they are heard and valued. This not only solves the current conflict but also strengthens the relationship, creating a base of trust and cooperation.

Emotional management is not the avoidance of conflict situations or inconvenient conversations; it is not the desire to please others much more because of the desire to please oneself less, or vice versa. Rather, it is not about hoarding power in the hands of the few but about having a platform where everyone is given a hearing and affirmed, and once decisions are arrived at, everyone should be given credit where it is due. Through an atmosphere of empathy, disagreements are not viewed as a way of winning or losing, and instead, there is a learning and growing process together.

CHAPTER 5

Empathy in the Workplace

EMPATHETIC LEADERSHIP

Empathetic leadership means that a great sense of understanding or feeling for other people enables you and makes them feel appreciated and understood. Such a leadership style does not imply adhering to all the requests or supporting all the feelings. Instead, it is the respect for the feelings and outlook of other team members; it is the recognition of their experiences, yet not necessarily agreeing with one another on all matters. This way, leaders are able to develop a culture of openness and trust, whereby workers are free to express themselves by giving their views and concerns without fear of losing their jobs and being victimized.

The process of seeking a perspective is at the core of empathetic leadership practice because it is a habit that spurs leaders to seek the opinions of their team members and consider them. This could be done by scheduling voice-of-the-team or roundtable meetings, where team members should be encouraged to express their opinions and emotions regarding projects and other happenings at the workplace. This not only supports team bonding but also enables individuals to empower themselves because they get the sense that they are part of the decision-making process.

Another important factor of empathetic leadership is setting boundaries. It entails the relay of decisions and policies in a manner that sustains trust and morale despite the fact that the information may not be pleasant. As an example, when a decision-maker must make a difficult decision or respond to a request with a negative answer, making these decisions in an empathic way means admitting the disappointment that the response will bring and encouraging others to comment or respond to concerns. Not only does this measure leave the admiral open to see the intelligence of the team, but it also leaves an impression that the leader cares about their emotional reactions.

Empathetic leaders likewise know how to maintain the equilibrium of empathy and authority. They realize that empathy is all about understanding others, but it does not imply declining control or power. Empathy helps good leaders move their teams through difficult situations, not only supporting them and listening but also clarifying expectations and calling team members to action. This is necessary in order to have a productive as well as a harmonious working environment.

The practice of empathetic leadership has been effective in real-world applications in different industries. As an example of working through the healthcare sector, the example of supervisors supervising workers through a shortage in staff and able to keep the working morale and output high by recognizing the stress and the strain on the current team and taking on a less threatening approach of asking more of the same overextended human resource is also possible. Likewise, in retail, when the turnover rate is very high in times of crisis, managers can retain employees by finding out what employees are worried about and collaborating with them in resolving their issues.

The subject of empathy in leadership practices is an inexhaustible topic, and it needs to be pursued through constant efforts and introspection. To evaluate the emotional climate in their team, leaders should perform empathy audits to find out the areas that they could improve. Such audits may locate the pain points that should otherwise remain unfounded and allow the leaders to resolve them beforehand, creating a more caring and supportive workplace culture.

The bottom line is that empathetic leadership is all about persuasion without making everyone converge. It is related to establishing an atmosphere in which people can feel comprehended and appreciated, which further leads to loyalty, innovation, and resourcefulness in the group. Leaders can encourage their respective teams to work toward resolving group challenges and support individual growth and satisfaction by learning the art of empathetic leadership.

BUILDING EMPATHETIC TEAMS

The quest to build empathetic teams starts with the built value of empathy within them. A culture of mutual respect, understanding, and collaboration can be rooted thanks to empathy in the team. Not only should people recognize one another as a feeling, but empathy should also be brought into everyday life and organizational life.

Empathy at the workplace is like a bonding mechanism between the team members, through which differences and conflicts are addressed with a common purpose. The empathetic team is founded on the capacity of active listening and giving a response that comes out of a profound comprehension. Here, the employee builds a new environment that allows team members to feel listened to and appreciated and promotes healthy conversations and the sharing of diverse opinions.

Implementing an effective strategy for developing empathetic teams implies conducting empathy audits on a regular basis. These audits measure the emotional team atmosphere, seeing where empathy is actually working well and where there may be some areas to develop. Teams can obtain a perspective on the position of members regarding empathy in interactions through anonymous surveys and feedback. Besides illuminating the lack of empathy, this procedure also discloses unanticipated pain points that can limit the bonding of the team.

Leadership is central to fostering empathy in the teams. Compassionate leaders lay the best example of how to behave on a team by being understanding and compassionate. They also empathize by confirming the feelings of those who are on the team, even when they may not identify with the points forwarded. It makes them feel their sense of belonging and creates trust that enables them to participate and be productive in a team.

The concept of empathetic leadership also entails observing the practice of perspective-seeking, which tends to orient leaders toward seeking opinions, listening to their team, and giving them thought. Leaders can ascertain that none of the voices will be left unheard and unconsidered when making any decision by constantly conducting rounds of tables of the voice of the team. This practice doubles as an act of improving empathy, morale, and motivation since members of a team will feel respected and that their input counts.

Embracing empathy in the team rituals may also be used to cement the importance of the concept. The team culture can be changed by simple measures like opening or closing the meeting with a gratitude round or checking on highs and lows. Such rituals help team members open up and share their personal experiences and feelings, promoting the relationship and better understanding.

In remote or hybrid teams, distance can cause a gap in empathy: to overcome these problems, digital-friendly rituals of empathy can be applied. Online "coffee breaks" and joint team diaries might help keep the feeling of belonging and understanding and not leave the members out of the process.

Finally, an effort to promote building empathetic teams should be based on the principle of never-ending learning and adapting. It entails being aware of and dealing with prejudice, accepting the range, and aiming at inclusive practices that respect the individuality of every member of the team. Amidst the challenges of the contemporary workplace setting, empathy develops into the essential mechanism of developing resilience, fostering performance, and realizing a successful shared outcome. Organizations can empower the process of team interaction with empathy and, thus, become a more humane and productive environment.

EMPATHY IN CUSTOMER RELATIONS

When it comes to customer relations, empathy becomes one of the most critical factors that has the potential to change a transaction into a meaningful encounter. The spirit of empathy here is that it creates the distance between a company and its customers and allows a much-needed consideration and mutual understanding that conventional strategies of customer service do not represent. This affiliation is no longer about fixing a problem or satisfying a need but distinguishing and confirming with the customer about his feelings, experience, and views.

When a customer contacts a company, it is more likely that his/her issues go beyond the apparent problem that is brought up. It can be an irritation over a late arrival of an order, a defective product, or a service that failed to measure up to expectations. But under these worries, there is another emotional layer of disappointment, the hope of the situation being resolved, and the desire to be heard and understood. Empathy will enable customer service representatives to strip off these layers and provide the customer with a response that will consider his or her emotional condition and solve the problem with authentic concern.

Customer relations require effective empathy, which involves active listening, which is a skill that requires one to be attentive and be able to give back to the customer what he or she has said. This not only makes the customer feel that their voice is being requested but also helps them get the real point behind their concern. As an example, a frustrated customer may become relieved when a certain problem is solved, but this may not be enough: a customer may have to feel that something has been done about his repeated complaint. An understanding attitude will include understanding their frustration, empathizing with them, and taking proactive measures to eliminate similar cases in the future.

In addition, customer relations empathy is personal. It entails personalizing the interactions to the specific needs of a customer. This may involve recalling what a particular customer told them before, what they like, or even his or her personal history, which will make him/her feel important and honored. It is through such customized communications that a negative customer can be transformed into a loyal brand champion since they develop an element of personal connection and loyalty to the brand.

Empowering the customer service teams to show empathy can be more than asking these folks to be nice or to be polite. It involves imparting knowledge of how the customer goes through his journey and how to design the moving emotions. Role-playing, empathy maps, and real-life situations can be useful in assisting the representatives in customer service to practice and develop their empathetic skills. Through this, they also get to know how to cope with complicated feelings and act in a manner that is both helpful and positive.

The effect of empathy in customer relations would not end in one-on-one relations. It may play an important role in the image and prosperity of a company. Customer satisfaction, a repeat purchase, and good word of mouth are the results of sympathetic customer service). In a modern age when customers can get access to a wide variety of choices, empathy can be one of the main differentiators that can make a company competitive towards its rivals.

It would safely say that when a customer relationship becomes an exercise in empathy, a transaction involving an exchange of goods and services becomes a relationship of mutual respect and understanding. It is the process of looking at the world through the eyes of the customer and reacting to it compassionately and with genuineness. However, by focusing on empathy, companies can not only address the immediate problems but also establish long-lasting relationships that would lead to long-term success.

HANDLING WORKPLACE CONFLICT

Understanding the complexities of workplace conflict cannot be approached in a simplistic way like resolution. It deals with the process of turning a possible discord into a chance to develop and learn. The core of such a change can be seen in the possibility of leveraging empathy as a means of breaking the boundaries and creating an innovation of teamwork.

In most formal contexts, conflict can be viewed in a negative light as it is regarded as a source of failure or dysfunctionality. But, in terms of empathy, conflict can be reconsidered as a drive towards creativity and innovation. It is possible to turn an opposing movement into an exploration of new ideas and opportunities by turning the confrontation into an opportunity.

This will start with active listening, which is one of the pillars of empathetic engagement. Listening and understanding other people's thoughts and feelings show reverence and affirmation, which is vital in calming down a situation. Here, we do not mean to listen to respond but to listen to understand in which the interests of each party can feel heard and respected.

After comprehension is derived, the next process to follow is a reflection of what has been heard. This reasoning not only attests to an understanding but also helps build trust. This makes the speaker understand that his or her point of view is being taken into serious consideration and is being listened to carefully. This step is critical in establishing a secure environment that makes every party free to share his or her ideas and feelings.

It takes quite some balancing between accommodation and assertion to respond with empathy. It entails listening to the emotions involved and trying to direct the discussion to positive results. This may include proposing concessions, offering innovative solutions, mediating alternative solutions, and addressing the needs and concerns of all stakeholders.

To simplify this process, a more structured framework model like the Listen, Reflect, respond model may prove to be very helpful. The model simulates the logical way of resolving the conflict, where every step of communication must be approached with attention and purposefulness. This framework encourages one to realize that the needs of other individuals should come first after the needs of oneself, and it motivates a person to look beyond the need to win as the main consideration and look at what one is trying to accomplish and how to do it out of collaboration and not contention.

In addition, empathy-based conflict resolution does not constitute a single intervention but a habit. It has to be a never-ending process of promoting a culture of openness and mutual respect. This consists of periodic check-ups, feedback cycles, and ceremonials that remind everyone that being empathetic is an essential organizational ethic.

In practice, both the leader and the team members would be helped by empathy training and workshops to provide them with the means of dealing with conflicts in the most productive manner possible. Examples of such programs may consist of emotional intelligence/resilience-building role-playing activities, emotional intelligence-building exercises assimilating empathy, mindfulness practices, etc.

After all, managing conflict at the workplace empathetically is not just about solving quarrels. It is not about creating an atmosphere where a free expression of different views is merely accepted but welcomed. Through the adoption of empathy as a strategic weapon, conflict can be a source of disunity. Instead, it may be intensified as a means of advancement and innovation. This transition not only makes teams work better but also adds to a more inclusive and peaceful working culture, a working environment where everyone can be heard, and every disagreement turns into a chance to arrange a closer connection and knowledge.

CHAPTER 6

Empathy and Society

EMPATHY IN COMMUNITY INITIATIVES

Empathy is a great activator in a community where empathy will create trust in various people and create unity. This sense of community often gets fostered with mutual rituals and practices that diminish differences and bias. These types of rituals, such as a book club, a neighborhood initiative, or an empathy walk, create a sense of belonging and some level of commonality of purpose. Such habitual activities not only promote the spirit of social empathy but are also a source of finding greater ties in communities.

The success of communal empathy rituals is due to the possibility of unifying people and making the experiences regular and important. As an example, one might consider monthly empathy book clubs with a different facilitator each month or neighborhood story swaps (a night when community members can share stories about their lives), where, by exchanging tales, people can gain a better understanding of others and thus connect them. These programs help people to communicate and listen to others, and this strengthens their level of respect and understanding of each other.

In addition, the empathy walks performed as a guided discussion with the local officials, elders, or new immigrants emphasize the value of hearing and learning other voices. These efforts not only make the community more inclusive but also empower members of the community to engage in the active creation of an empathetic environment. The founding of such initiatives, however, means that there is a need to ensure the sustainment of such initiatives by tackling resistance or apathy among groups. Distributing leadership assignments and carrying out anonymous opinion surveys can assist in ensuring continual involvement and inclusiveness so that each voice is listened to and considered valuable.

Real cases of success exist in areas where the principle of empathy-driven initiatives has been carried out. An example is that a block association can facilitate neighborhood conflicts by engaging in an empathy circle regularly where residents meet and open up about the issue they have in an empathetic way. Likewise, schools could adopt a so-called buddy system that would match students from diverse backgrounds and promote friendship and comprehension.

All these practices exemplify how empathetic behavior can make a change within the community. Communities focused on empathy will enjoy supportive community conditions whereby trust, cooperation, and shared objectives are achieved. These initiatives can always be measured after the effects, and people have been living with reduced conflicts, enhanced cooperation, and more cohesiveness. Empathy enables not just the local communities to solve immediate problems. Still, it prepares them to become self-sustainable and self-sufficient in the long-term as well, such as through achieving social harmony.

EMPATHY IN EDUCATION

The world of education is no exception, as empathy can be viewed as a revolutionary aspect that can sculpt the dynamics of the learning process and have a profound influence on the way students are transformed into people of conscience and social responsibility. Empathy is not only a soft skill in terms of teaching and interaction in classrooms but also a fundamental element that promotes teaching performance and involvement of students. The development of empathy in the educational environment starts with acknowledging varying student needs and establishing an inclusive educational environment in which every student should feel appreciated and listened to.

Teachers play a critical role in empathizing modeling. This would make a lot of a difference in classrooms because they could empathize with the emotions of students and also help students with their emotions. The empathic mode creates a very supportive learning environment where students can feel free to talk about themselves and are even invited to be more perceptive of the material. Empathetic teachers are more capable of recognizing the personal issues of every individual student, which enables them to design their teaching method based on the needs of a particular child, thus enhancing the educational process's performance.

Empathy in education is not only in the teacher-student relationship. It also includes peer interactions where learners are taught to work with other views and acquire skills that will enable them to be good team players. Educators can use perspective-taking skills by making students perform tasks that will allow them to learn more about their peers and their feelings. It is a practice that not only improves social cohesion in the classroom but also makes them ready to deal with a diverse and connected world that lies outside the school premises.

In addition, empathy in education plays a critical role in conflict-addressing and reduction. When faced with situations where dissent cannot be avoided, empathy can be used to resolve the same. It allows people to approach conflicts in a manner that is consistent with knowledge and respect and transform any possible disruption into an experience and learning. Educators can facilitate the use of empathy to calm down situations and create a smoother learning atmosphere by organizing a scaffolded learning process and free discussions with the students.

The addition of empathy in the curriculum can also greatly impact the emotional intelligence of the students. Social-emotional learning (SEL) programs focus on teaching empathy and other essential abilities, including self-awareness and emotion regulation. The programs also buttress students with the means by which they can get a better picture of their feelings, as well as the feelings of their fellow people, which can establish a basis in which they can better healthily relate to others.

Moreover, sympathy in education equips the young ones with future leadership duties. Empathetic leaders will be in a better position to inspire and motivate others, work with diversity in teams, and build an inclusionary community. Teachers, through their early instillation of the importance of empathy, precondition students into becoming prudent and efficient leaders in any sphere.

The effectiveness of empathy in teaching is corroborated by evidence showing that teaching that involves empathy leads to increased educational outputs in terms of both academic performance and well-being. Students who learn in caring environments have been found to be highly driven to learn, better disciplined, as well as feel better about themselves. These positive results correspond to the significance of integrating empathy into school systems.

The conclusion is that incorporating empathy in learning is not a luxury; it is a must in raising well-balanced human beings who can then make constructive contributions to society. As educators, students, and educational institutions learn to empathize, they create a culture of understanding and compassion jointly, which leads to the possibility of an empathetic and interconnected world.

EMPATHY IN HEALTHCARE

Empathy as a concept proves vital in the practice of healthcare as it forms a pillar in establishing adequate interactions with patients and providing acceptable forms of care. This importance cannot be overestimated, as it constitutes the foundation for the development of trust and rapport between healthcare experts and their patients. Empathy in health care is way beyond a feeling; rather, it is a vital communication ability that helps in the accuracy of diagnosis, patient compliance, and satisfaction.

The willingness to empathize with a patient in a hospital setting means putting yourself in the patient's position, being able to picture yourself in their shoes and care about their feelings, and being able to show compassion. This means not merely hearing what the patient is saying, but it means healthcare personnel hearing what is not necessarily said. This would permit a more in-depth comprehension of the status of the patient and make possible a better and more customized treatment strategy.

To healthcare providers, empathy is a complex ability that integrates mental, emotional, and compassionate factors. Cognitive empathy entails the intellectual skills of reading the situation and the perspective of a patient.

Emotional empathy can be contrasted as it enables caregivers to relate to the emotions of the patient, and as a result, it creates a common emotionally experienced state. Caring empathy takes it a decipher further, not only learning to keep along and to share the sentiment but even going an extra step to assist the patient. In another example, a nurse can realize that the patient is suffering and not only vocalize what they can do about it but act, as well, providing relief by fixing a pillow or by offering a comforting hand.

Caring in healthcare is especially crucial to the improvement of patient outcomes. It was demonstrated that understanding patients and how they feel will encourage them to follow treatment plans and provide essential information regarding symptoms. Such collaboration can result in increased accuracy of diagnosis as well as treatment. In addition, faithful encounters with a patient may tremendously help relieve anxiety and tension in the patient, making the healthcare process more positive.

The empathetic approach may be difficult but paramount in a situation of extreme stress, like in an emergency or intensive care unit. In such an environment, medical workers are frequently under time and stressful conditions, so it may not be easy to interact empathically. Nevertheless, even a short period of empathy may bring a substantial result. Just a recognition that a patient is afraid or uncomfortable is enough to relax the anxiety and create a feeling of security and care.

The empathy aspect is also a decisive factor in the mental health of medical practitioners. Working by being empathetic may prove to be emotionally draining, which is referred to as empathy fatigue. It is a state of being emotionally drained and having a low capacity to relate to other people, especially those who work in the field of caregiving. To reduce this, healthcare facilities are increasingly viewing empathy training and self-care programs as important tools that help the providers retain their emotional strength and keep providing compassionate care.

In addition, empathy in health care goes beyond specific communication with patients. It includes a wider promise of realizing and dealing with issues of the system that influence the care of patients, like cultural competence and health disparities. It is suggested that healthcare providers should maintain a continuous process of learning and reflection in the spirit of improving their capacity to relate to different races of patients.

To sum up, empathy is an inseparable part of productive medical practice. It is useful in improving the patient experience, clinical outcomes, and the emotional well-being of the provider. A culture of empathy in the healthcare systems would mean that the services not only proved to be clinically competent but also highly humane and sensitive to the demands of the patients.

EMPATHY IN SOCIAL JUSTICE

In the framework of social justice, the concept of empathy can become a truly powerful instrument that would decrease the distance between different communities and help create a sense of unity out of diversity. It is more than a purely emotional cognition into a means of gaining an important foothold and transformation. Empathy requires personal dedication to listening, learning, and working towards means that truly empower marginalized voices. This involvement is the fundamental formation of allyship since the intentions are not enough, as the actions should be consistent and represent actual solidarity.

In social justice, empathy calls for individuals to face their privileges and biases in the world and to fight together on shared platforms and in shared spaces with the people and groups who have historically been silenced or ignored. It demands an ideological transformation of the pretentious state of performative allyship, which is more of a self-proclaiming and self-satisfying attitude to the authenticity of advocacy that is also coherent and influential. This change is not simple and relaxed, as it presupposes unlearning some established prejudices and assumptions, which create systemic inequalities.

One of the primary strategies for enhancing empathy in social justice is creating a conducive atmosphere where the less fortunate get a chance to speak and suffer no disruption or watering down of their voices. It is crucial to say that listening circles and inclusive meetings or events are crucial in this regard since underrepresented voices are given the opportunity to perform. This not only confirms their experiences but also enables them to have leverage in decisions and actions that affect their lives.

Empathy is also important in eliminating political and cultural differences that are full of emotional risks and discomforts. In cross-divide conversations, one must be bold enough and ready to accept the fear of making something go wrong. The models of empathy, including the Listen, Reflect, and Respond models, can be useful in the de-escalation of a stiff conversation and turning the situation into curiosity rather than conversion. Ask open questions such as what life situations influenced your perception towards it. Promotes the opportunity to learn and relate even in the event of difference.

Another required element of empathetic involvement in social justice is establishing boundaries. One should know when it is beneficial and efficient to cease a discussion or other kinds of communication so as to ensure the safety of one's mental health without closing all the doors to future communication. It could be accomplished through remarks such as I want to continue learning with you. However, I need a break on this subject at this moment.

There are many life examples of successful allyship and empathy demonstrated in practice; this demonstrates the strength of these principles in various settings. These are the real-life examples of when empathy-based programs have resulted in significant improvements: when employee resource groups introduced mentorship programs, parents insisted on accommodating inclusive school policies, and so on. The potential of empathy as a tool of social justice is manifested in the experiences of volunteers whose offerings of their skills in furthering the cause of grassroots movements to gain equity, like the immigrant rights movements, are invaluable processes.

Finally, empathy in social justice requires not only deepening such understanding of other people but also going beyond intellect and taking specific action against injustices and inequalities. It requires continuing learning and doing and asks individuals and groups to work towards a more inclusive and equitable world constantly. By understanding one another, we can bridge the gap between them, creating equal and full representation in our society.

CHAPTER 7

Empathy Across Cultures

CULTURAL VARIATIONS IN EMPATHY

Empathy has become a complicated issue in the complex tapestry of human interaction as it is a kind of connective tissue in the interrelation of people and a complex puzzle when it is considered in terms of cultural diversity. The definition of empathy, or rather the ability to share and comprehend the emotions of another person, is vastly different across cultures and depends on the social rules, communication patterns, and the existing strongly established values.

Empathy in most Western cultures may be represented in the form of direct, expressive language and emotions. Such groups are prone to appreciate openness and open expression of feelings, whereby empathy is provoked through active listening and verbal confirmation. Comparatively,

Eastern cultures may give precedence to empathy, which is manifested in non-verbal communication and less direct knowledge about the feelings of a different person. In this case, empathy is usually to read between the lines and interpret the unsaid, and it is rather geared towards harmony and not being direct.

The concept of face in most Asian societies, such as the aspect of saving face and respect, is prominent in socializing. In this case, empathy, to some extent, includes a precise balance between considering emotions and avoiding the loss of face of the other party. This may necessitate a subtle undertone where empathy can be expressed not by words but by deeds, such as being supportive without highlighting the weakness of the individual.

Besides, the influence of collectivism and individualism is important to determine the manifestation of empathy. Empathy in collectivist cultures, which exist in Latin America or some African countries, goes beyond immediate groups and symptoms and refers to a widely perceived society as good. In this case, caring behaviors are much related to collective harmony and social responsibilities. In some African societies, to give an example, the belief of Ubuntu, which takes into consideration the rights of the community over the individual, has a sense of collective empathy as they believe the need of the community beats the subjective want.

Conversely, those individualistic cultures, such as in North America and Western Europe, may be more concerned with regard to empathy and instead center it towards the personal emotional experience and self-expression. Applying labels in these societies, when one develops the capacity to express his/her feelings, can be viewed as an indicator of empathetic interaction that facilitates personal and direct empathy.

The problem of cross-cultural differences is the fact that there is always a possibility of cross-cultural misunderstanding in the interactions between representatives of different backgrounds. What may have been interpreted as a show of empathy in a given culture may mean something different in another culture. As an example, the Western culture of making eye contact during a conversation to show that a person is being attended to and sympathetic may be deemed as showing disrespect to the culture that preaches modesty and acts in a deferential manner.

As a way of developing authentic cross-cultural empathy, developing cultural humility, which can be interpreted as sensitivity to learning about the cultural milieu of others, is essential. This entails acknowledging and accepting differences in ways of demonstrating empathy and being open-minded to adjust the way of doing it according to the needs of various people. Some practical suggestions could be that open-ended questions should be asked in order to learn more about cultural norms, and one should be mindful of non-verbal actions that are being interpreted as a sign of empathy across various cultures.

Finally, learning to be empathetic to other cultural differences makes us more knowledgeable about human association. Not only will these help us deepen our relationships with others in many ways, but they also allow us to develop a more understanding and accepting global society.

EMPATHY IN GLOBAL COMMUNICATION

In international communication, empathy turns out to be the critical element that breaks all cultural, linguistic, and geographical boundaries. Being capable of getting into the skin of other people is not just a personal tool of the person but a very important element in promoting international collaboration and comprehension. That is why, with the interconnection of the world, the necessity of empathetic communication is growing stronger than ever.

In international communication, empathy means subtle admiration of cultural diversity and interest in listening to views other than those that we generally embrace. It involves the willingness to learn and be changed by realizing that communication style, values, and expectations may differ greatly depending on culture. Acceptance of such differences enables people and institutions to construct bridges, as opposed to walls, to engage more fruitfully in interaction.

Otherwise, active listening and good listening styles are among the most important features of empathy in international communication. It refers not only to hearing but also to understanding the situation of the words that are heard and the feelings that go with them. It is a matter of the existence of existence in a discussion, about being involved, interested, and concerned about the opinion of the person. The said listening is a central tenet of trust and respect, which is indispensable to successfully overcoming communication barriers between cultures.

Besides, there is some potential level of flexibility and adaptability of empathy in global communication. It has the desire to modify communication style in order to accommodate cultural parameters and expectations of the relevant party more effectively. This may entail changing the language, tone, or even channel of communication so that it is clearly understood. This malleability is not the issue of denying oneself identity but finding common ground where both can come to grips with their mutual understanding.

Emotional awareness when communicating globally may take several forms in real life. As an example, one can observe the attempts of multinational corporations to customize their marketing strategies to the local cultures. One can also note it in planning diplomacy in international relations because diplomats have to operate in complicated cultural fields in order to develop cooperation and settle conflicts. In both situations, it is important to be able to see both sides of the story so as to arrive at desirable results.

In addition, one can use empathy in international interchange beyond words. Knowledge of non-verbal communication or body language and facial expressions also enunciates empathy and understanding. Being sensitive to such signals can help increase the effectiveness of communication to a great extent so that one can react to the moods and motives of others positively.

The aspect of empathy in international communication can also be seen in the digital era when technology has facilitated cross-border interactions as never before. Although digital platforms are enormous sources of connection, they may also have drawbacks, i.e., they may lead to misinterpretation, and they lack the physical aspect. In this case, empathy is even more important because communicators have to remember the tone and aim of their written communication and make their intentions as friendly as possible despite the absence of face-to-face communication.

Global communication is all about having empathy and the feeling that all of us are united humans. It is about understanding that all of us, although different in some ways, share the same needs and aspirations. Through empathetic insight, everyone and every organization will be in a position to make the world less tense and less alienated by using communication as a medium of connection instead of division. Such an empathetic style not only contributes to better personal and professional relationships but also opens the door to more inclusive and long-term global interactions.

INCLUSIVE EMPATHY PRACTICES

Inclusive empathy is a strategy that aims to highlight that empathy activities should be adjusted to reflect neurodiversity, disability, and cross-cultural differences throughout the world. This notion considers the fact that empathy is not a ring-shaped answer and should be a flexible practice that should be adapted to fit the needs of different individuals and communities. Inclusive empathy is about being flexible, humbling, and creative through its co-creation, which makes a significant difference between standardized and individualized empathy techniques.

In a bid to establish real affiliation among the various neurotypes, surefire ways have been identified to connect well through communication and the formation of memorable associations. This incorporates such elements as the usage of the so-called clear and concrete language that is especially effective in the case of autistic or neurodivergent people. Communication can also be improved by giving written prompts rather than depending on verbal sharing and opening it to people who process information differently. These strategies not only make understanding an easy process but also generate an atmosphere in which all the participants feel valued and respected.

Practices that involve being culturally sensitive to empathy also exemplify the role that acknowledgment and respect for cultural diversity play in the expression of empathy. Both non-Western, Indigenous, and collectivistic communities have rituals and expectations applied to empathy practices. Such rituals as group-based affirmation in African or Asian cultures, consensus-building through Indigenous talking circles, etc., can become a strong illustration of how empathy may be expressed and experienced cross-culturally. The mentioned practices also explain why cultural sensitivity and awareness are critical in the context of empathy work, so empathy is not just inclusive but also magnificently respectful of various traditions and values.

Availability and consent are an essential component of inclusive empathy in whatever empathy is done. This entails providing the framework for building inclusive groups and digital environments to welcome different talents and inclinations. An example given here would be sending agendas or questions beforehand and, therefore, giving them sufficient processing time to contribute to a more inclusive environment. Also, it is important to make both physical and online locations accessible to people with different abilities so that a visit or an activity could be an inclusive experience.

Inclusive empathy can put the practitioners in a state where they have to depart from the classical model of empathy and adopt a more elaborate and specific model. It welcomes embracing the knowledge of individual and cultural differences, welcoming to be more empathetic, and considering such everyday practices to be truly inclusive and empowering to both parties. Inclusive empathy practices come at the forefront of creating a more authentic and meaningful relationship within divergent communities because a priority on accessibility coupled with consent and cultural sensitivity provides the avenues to build a connection beyond stereotypes. These practices not only ensure better understanding and cooperation but also a feeling of belonging and mutual respect, which are part and parcel of any successful community.

EMPATHY IN INTERNATIONAL RELATIONS

The circumstances in the rather complicated world of international relations have resulted in empathy taking on the role of a revolutionary agent that has the potential to erase all boundaries and initiate collaboration despite cultural and political differences. This subtle art deals with the art of knowing others based on emotions, and in my fields of global diplomacy and relations, this is vital.

In the case of international relations, empathy does not only demand an emotional response to other cultures; it also demands a cognitive appreciation of foreign contexts as well as historical backgrounds. International negotiators and other diplomats regularly deal with their counterparts who belong to a very different cultural milieu. In this case, empathy will enable them to predict the reaction and determine the personal motivations that may be unnoticed. By picking up the hidden emotions and cultural stories, the diplomats will be able to work in a negotiation process with the nuance that makes people trust one another and less prone to conflict.

In addition, empathy in this sphere is not only about individual relationships but also as far as systemic insights. It entails the identification and correction of the historical injustices and socio-economic inequality that tend to form the basis of tensions between countries. As an example, it is possible to recognize the historical effects of colonialism or economic exploitation to open a more equal and respectful conversation. Under this strategy, it is important to engage in listening and understanding the accounts that influence the position of a nation and subsequently draw solutions that are sustainable and peaceful.

Applied to international affairs, empathy can be used and may be placed in different forms of diplomatic efforts and activities. An example of such powerful tools that can be used in the promotion of empathy is cultural exchange. When nations experience one another's culture, they can have an understanding of each other that is beyond the political course. The exchanges will encourage people to feel a feeling of shared humanity, which is necessary for establishing long-term international relationships.

The other way is to institutionalize empathy in international organizations and forums. Cultural sensitivity and emotional intelligence training programs are becoming very important. The skills taught through such programs will enable those participating in diplomatic affairs and other international stakeholders to handle different stakeholders sympathetically. This kind of training can not only improve the personal relations between people but also lead to a more sympathetic institutional culture, which can become the cause of a change in global policies.

There are no challenges, though, to stimulating empathy in international relations. It needs to conquer deeply rooted inclinations and prejudices that may prevent free dialogue. Actors in diplomacy should not be afraid to challenge these prejudices and develop an open mind on new ideas. It is a habit that mostly requires a personal inspection of cultural presumptions in oneself and an ability always to learn more.

Conclusively, it is fair to say that empathy is a very vital element in the toolbox of international relations. It provides a new way of thinking and cooperation that is vitally necessary in the process of dealing with the intricate issues that the modern world is facing. Focusing on empathy, international actors will be able to develop a more inclusive and collaborative world environment, leading to peace and prosperity for both parties. Empathy is an essential concept that can be used to turn the perceived negativity of world relations into positive outcomes of realization and development as countries move forward in the culture of international relations.

CHAPTER 8

Challenges to Empathy

EMPATHY FATIGUE

The issue we are going to consider is called empathy fatigue, which appears as an invisible enemy in the sphere of caregiving and helping professions. This type of fatigue cannot be considered one of the general stresses or burnouts because it is related to the particular loss of emotional resources due to constant contact with the sufferings of other people. In the beginning, it manifests itself as something rather disguised; it sneaks in through physical, emotional, and behavioral cues, which can be quite easily overlooked as ordinary fatigue. There are such symptoms as general fatigue, aggression, depression, indifference, and even somatic problems such as headaches. They are indicators that point to the necessity of providing some intervention before the breaking point is reached.

To comprehend empathy fatigue, it is essential to make a difference between this term and ordinary stress. Although stress is an ordinary aspect of life, empathy fatigue is a distinct condition that does not emphasize the physical aspects of empathy. It causes certain interventions that answer the emotional and psychological needs to which people involved in empathetic occupations or jobs are expected. Acknowledging the existence of this difference is important as it will help to emphasize the necessity of using specific forms of support rather than traditional approaches to stress relief.

A self-identification tool or self-checklist may prove very helpful in this regard. Such a tool makes one reflective and pushes the idea of early intervention by asking: "Do I find interactions I once found enjoyable dreaded?" or, Am I getting to be cynical or resentful? All these reflective questions will assist these individuals in realizing the emotional status they are in and ensure taking the first initiative regarding recovery.

Short-term treatments of empathy fatigue entail adopting the habits of reset rituals and fast interventions. Small details such as having a 10-minute solo walk following emotionally challenging appointments or putting a 24-hour communication shutdown following exhausting interactions are sufficient to bring immediate relief. These are some mental resets when one has lost all one's emotional balance and needs to think things through with a new wind.

To remedy this situation, it is critical to implement an active path, and such should include daily, weekly, and monthly regimens that would maintain emotional health. Mindful breathing, gratitude journaling, short exercises, and daily practices may be performed every day. In contrast, some peer support meetings or an hour of digital disconnection may be carried out once a week. Professional life or monthly reflections are also very essential to keep the feeling on track.

The Prevention of Fatigue Toolkit of Empathy is all-inclusive and conveys scientifically endorsed regimens and guidelines based on research in psychology, neuroscience, and well-being. This toolkit indicates that consistency is of great importance, which is proved by the facts and examples of cases where frequent assistance practices are more effective than crisis interventions.

Moreover, the toolkit presents lists and graphics to track habits, which will allow people to develop and maintain new habits with less effort. Individual and group testimonials and narrations show how these practices changed their characters and provide inspiration and visualization of the concrete gains of active empathy management.

Finally, to combat empathy fatigue, one should identify the symptoms, initiate the recovery process, and prevent a negative state. This way, people are able to preserve their emotional reserves and the ability to empathize, and they can keep on helping other people in a long-term and efficient way.

OVERCOMING EMPATHY BARRIERS

Empathy is a connecting force that secures people in the context of human interaction because it binds those with different backgrounds and experiences. However, some maladies hinder the natural relationship between people, and the walls usually block such a bridge. By being aware of these barriers, it is possible to slowly start breaking them down, enabling a more natural and much-needed empathy.

Bias, whether conscious or unconscious, is one of the most widespread fences to empathy. Prejudice affects the way we think and the manner in which we relate to others, resulting in misunderstanding and misanalysis. It creates a barrier that we cannot overcome and does not go in the way of empathy because it distorts our image of the world. The means to counter this is to practice self-reflection and actively attempt to discover our own biases and dispel them as well. The definition of evaluating the present state of prejudice is an assessment that can be employed in this aspect quite the same as the implicit association tests to expose the deeply rooted prejudices that necessitate personal development.

The other issue is the digital divide, which typifies what is now a major part of communication. At a time when relationships are frequently conducted behind screens, the lack of nonverbal expressions may result in misunderstanding and the inability to feel. One has to learn to use digital empathy, meaning a tone and intention awareness when writing a message. Even online, misunderstandings can be reduced with simple behaviors like reading back what one has written, as well as being empathetic in their language choice.

The notion of conflict also presents a bigger threat to the concept of empathy. Generally, when conflict sets in, the usual response becomes defensive, where winning takes precedence over comprehension. However, conflict may be viewed as a chance to empathize by using some approaches and strategies that involve listening and understanding but not responding only. Such frames as the Listen, Reflect Respond model help to remind the individual that it is important to value empathy over ego, and, instead of possible discord, it can become a foundation of further knowledge.

There are both external and internal aspects of empathy barriers, and they can be summed up as emotional exhaustion and burnout. Empathy fatigue is one of the problems in the high-emotional labor profession because it results in distance and loss of empathic ability. To avoid empathy fatigue, it is necessary to perform active self-care measures, i.e., establishing borders and regularly engaging in self-reflection to be emotionally resilient.

Also, empathetic interactions may be disturbed by cultural differences. Differences in communication modes, social customs, and emotional displays may cause misunderstandings. The development of a specific cultural humility can contribute to the empathy between other groups and avoid the risk of cultural ignorance. Cultural humility is a realization that learning about the cultures of other people is a lifelong process. This means open-mindedness, curiosity, and openness to the views, not accepting that being empathetic needs only an intention; it needs action and adjustment to the situation.

Last but not least, perfectionism might impede empathy by perpetrating unrealistic emotional expectations. Perfectionist tendencies in empathy will cause frustrations and evasion in instances when it fails to live up to expectations. This pressure can be eased by accepting imperfection coupled with the realization that empathy is a skill that develops and improves with usage and experience.

These barriers can never be overcome once and for all, but rather, the process of growth and adaptation is ongoing. By being aware of these hurdles and working on them, people will be able to improve their empathy, thereby establishing stronger and more fulfilling relationships in every aspect of their lives.

EMPATHY AND TECHNOLOGY

This is the case in the contemporary set-up where technology has brought man closer together and, therefore, affected the expression and reception of empathy. Digital communication tools are raising new issues and challenges in regard to empathy. The lack of nonverbal communication is one of the major challenges when trying to perfect digital empathy because it is imperative to interpret a wide variety of emotions and motifs. Face-to-

Face In a face-to-face conversation, body language, tone of voice, and face exhibition are enough to give context that is lacking in texts and email messages. This contextual deformity may bring confusion where the text is deprived of the details that would carry an empathic message.

New forms of empathetic communication should be established in the virtual landscape so that this virtual world can become significantly more compassionate. One of the suggestions is to be more deliberate about what we say and use digital mediums, i.e., emojis and punctuation, to express the tone. These details are tiny, but they can make a difference between a cold message and a warm and thoughtful one. Furthermore, checking messages one more time before sending them may be a good idea as it may help to make sure that the tone used is transparent and, consequently, decreases the risk of a misinterpretation.

Timing is the other crucial element of digital empathy. This responsiveness of online communication is, at times and in certain cases, an instance of being hasty and unthoughtful, which can be construed as dismissive and insensitive. Often, a few seconds of reflection with a pause before reacting is possible to create more mature and compassionate interaction. Also, it is good practice to confirm that you have received a message when you cannot be in a position to give a complete reply after receiving a message, as doing so shows that you are considerate of the time and feelings of the other person.

Possibly, in spite of these challenges, technology also brings with it unprecedented opportunities for empathy. It makes it possible to network on a huge scale, and individuals get to share their experiences and points of view; social media networks, e.g., can make voices and stories louder and create understanding and compassion between different communities. However, all this potential is fulfilled only by the time the users of these platforms approach these systems consciously and with a focus on substance rather than artificial relations.

Digital empathy is also required to be familiar with the dynamic of intent versus impact. The absence of contextual clues means that some messages that are supposed to be supportive are being interpreted either as intrusive or even inappropriate. Therefore, one should ensure that we are open to constructive criticism and even be ready to change our communication styles. It is not too hard to apologize without explanation when something is misinterpreted, and we must specify what we meant with an arrived system of being empathetic as well.

Also, online sources can be used to establish a place of empathy-based communication. The use of online forums and discussion groups allows individuals to discuss various topics that may move a person beyond their bias. Interactions of this type can be organized in a way that fosters empathy through the establishment of rules that facilitate respectful listening and sharing.

To conclude, even though technology poses a threat to empathy, it also provides people with the means and possibilities to improve it. Through mind-conscious communication and the connection-enhancing capabilities of digital platforms, we can find a way to create a network of empathetic people that is not limited to physical and cultural distance. With the further penetration of technology into our lives, digital empathy will play a significant role in developing mutual understanding and empathy in the world with a rising number of interrelations.

EMPATHY IN CRISIS SITUATIONS

During times of emergency, the capacity to be empathic turns out not only helpful but also critical. Whether personal or collective, crisis introduces people into a condition of exaggerated vulnerability and emotional unsteadiness. Empathy is aimed at holding things together in such a time; empathy provides relief and understanding in times of chaos and fear. These are the times when the real power of empathy becomes visible since it helps to overcome emotional gaps that have evolved in crises.

The initial thing to do when using empathy during a crisis is to identify the emotional terrain of the affected. There is a wide range of affections involved in crises, which entails fear, anger, confusion, and grief, and the reaction to each one of them requires an empathetic but refined reaction. Becoming aware of the particular emotions involved enables the targeted approach, one that acknowledges the personal experience of the person and can give him or her the feeling of being heard and understood. Such validation is essential since it aids in the reduction of isolation and powerlessness, which are prevalent feelings in crisis cases.

Active listening is a skill that is also needed in giving empathy during a crisis because listening does not only involve hearing what people say but also comprehending their emotions. It is being completely alive, providing attention without distraction and patience. In such situations, active listening can be taken to avoid the temptation to offer quick solutions or reassurances and, instead, concentrate on showing an individual that the emotions and experiences that the individual went through are understood. This strategy can create an enabling environment where people can express themselves without fear of judgment or rejection.

The other important element of empathy during crises is the support without touching on the boundaries too much. It entails the provision of supportive care in a way that is linked to the loss of autonomy and dignity of the caring individual. Questions should be asked as to what kind of assistance is required instead of presuming, and this makes a person more powerful as he will feel in control of the situation. Being empathetic, in this meaning, is being aware of partnership and collaboration, pulling together through the crisis.

Furthermore, an empathetic approach to crisis should be flexible because not all situations and people respond to the same approach. The manner in which empathy should be communicated is influenced by cultural factors, personal factors, and situational factors. An understanding of such differences and acting on them based on susceptibility is a feature of a truly empathetic interaction. It is this flexibility that makes empathy useful and substantive and not generic nor perfunctory.

Having empathy is also important when it comes to developing resiliency in crises. Emotional support and knowing what somebody is going through are important aspects of empathy as they assist people in developing the strength to deal with negative experiences. It brings optimism and its potential to people who need to be told that they are not alone and that their experience is vital. Such an environment can be an effective force of change and recovery, and one can see one come out of a crisis with a fresh purpose and belonging.

Finally, empathy during crises involves establishing a human bond beyond the present situation. It reminds us that we are all human and that acts of compassion and goodwill may be the only respite during times of trouble. When empathy is welcomed, we not only help others in their desperate hour but also make our lives richer, developing a keener insight into what life is like and the ultimate value of kindness and understanding.

CHAPTER 9

Empathy for Personal Growth

EMPATHY AND EMOTIONAL INTELLIGENCE

Empathy is a key tool in the complex dance of interacting with other people. It thus serves as a turning point between emotional intelligence and its application in the multiple spheres of life. It is not just a character trait, but it is a developed skill, one that is developed with a bit of practice. With empathy, we are able to see how others feel and sense what they are thinking, and this forms a blanket of intuition and relationship beyond just talking.

Emotional intelligence, which is mostly characterized by self-awareness, self-regulation, motivation, empathy, and social skills, forms the ground over which empathy is established. It is in such a light that empathy ends up being such a mighty instrument as it helps people travel complicated emotional patterns with style and gentleness. Emotional intelligence forms the basis of understanding oneself and others' feelings, whereas empathy is the method by which these feelings are admitted and respected.

A mindful and conscious attitude takes over the development of empathy. It demands open-mindedness and the desire to relate with other people on an emotional level. This interaction is not passive or a one-way dialogue; it is a listening, observing, and responding process. It is through empathy that one can walk into another person and see the things they see and feel as they feel. Mutual interpretation leads to feelings of belonging and acceptance, which are essential elements of emotional health.

Empathy can take a number of forms in practice. It is reflected in the moments of silent encouragement rendered to a friend in trouble, in the forbearing tolerance administered to a colleague in a tight spot, or in the sympathetic aid given to some stranger in distress. All these are not big gestures of empathy but more of small (but consistent) actions that create a sense of trust and respect.

The development of empathy also means getting rid of obstacles. These obstacles may be internal (biases, prejudices, etc.) or external (cultural differences, problems with communications, and so on). Being aware of and dealing with such barriers will help one improve their empathetic skills and build more inclusive and supportive surroundings.

In addition, empathy is an important factor in leadership and teamwork. When empathetic leaders exercise their high degree of empathy, they are capable of influencing and engaging their personnel and instilling a culture of team building and innovations. Empathetic leaders know what the team members want and what bothers them, and this knowledge results in more effective communication and solving an issues. Empathy helps in cooperation, and conflict decreases in a team since the team members are more likely to value and respect one another.

The use of empathy does not start and finish at the level of people's relationships with others; it is also applicable to creating change in society. As the world grows more and more divided along the lines of differences, empathy is one of the unifying factors that have helped foster understanding and compassion across cultures and ideologies. It makes citizens want to advocate and apply social justice and embrace oppressed communities, and a little wave of change will make a big impact.

But in the end, empathy is a force of change. It adds value to human experiences as well as improves emotional intelligence levels, enabling people to relate to others profoundly and learn to operate within the multi-faceted life of life with compassion and wisdom. By building empathy, we are also able to increase our emotional health of ourselves, but as we build, the world we live in becomes more understanding and compassionate.

DEVELOPING EMPATHY SKILLS

One of the main pillars of human interaction and communication is empathy, which is a skill that may be developed with conscious effort and mindfulness practice. It is more than just sympathy, which involves the active connection to the experiences and emotions of others. In order to learn empathy skills, the first thing is to learn about the multifaceted nature of empathy, which involves cognitive, emotional, and compassionate empathy. All these aspects are important in the way we feel and respond to the world around us.

Cognitive empathy is basically an ability to understand what another person might be thinking or feeling by considering his or her mental state or way of seeing a situation. This is an important component of empathy that can be used in establishing connections between opposing positions because it causes one to be open-minded and also minimizes misconceptions.

Cognitive empathy can be improved through activities that are based on perspective-taking, like reading different stories or performing role-play games that require them to think from a different perspective.

Emotional empathy, however, has more to do with sharing the feelings of another person. It is the capability of sensing what another person is going through emotionally, and this forms a visceral bond in the process of understanding and empathizing. Individuals can nurture emotional empathy by listening actively to one another, which means being totally focused, understanding, responding, and remembering what is being communicated. This is not only used to recognize the emotions of other people but also to legitimize experiences without interpreting them as right or wrong.

The next level of empathy is compassionate empathy, which is the ability not only to understand what other people are feeling and share their feelings but also to experience the urge to assist others in case of their need. It is the element of empathy that spurs us to action and is useful in social change, such as in intra-personal relations, and it is, therefore, a strong tool for social change. Compelled empathy with compassion would be an outcome that would be accomplished by volunteering, attending to the community, or just being there in a friendly way by supporting one of his friends and family.

Self-reflection and self-awareness are also important aspects of empathy skill development. Considering our emotional reactions and prejudices can help us to know more about how these might influence our communications with other individuals by simply pondering about them on a consistent basis. Such mindfulness activities as journaling or meditation might help improve self-awareness, and as a result, one will be able to interpret situations in a more empathetic, non-reactive way.

Besides, empathy is also something that can be developed on a daily basis through micro-practices that can be smoothly incorporated into a person's routine. Empathetic understanding can easily be elevated through simple random acts of kindness such as gratitude and the offer to act as a listening ear. These exercises are tiny, but when combined, they lead to a more understanding attitude and character.

A way of ensuring that empathy becomes part of daily life entails the ability to identify and overcome obstacles, including personal prejudice and emotional exhaustion. It involves dedication to lifelong learning and changes and the consent to have hard talks, an open heart, and an open brain. With these challenges, one can have more profound and natural relationships with the people around.

Finally, empathy is a continuous process in which one builds a more profitable relationship in both the professional and personal lives. It provides people with the strength to find common ground with one another, building a feeling of community and respect for one another. With concerted effort and thought, empathy can be made to seem a whole and healthy aspect of a person, benefiting both personal as well as social health.

EMPATHY IN SELF-REFLECTION

During times in silence, when a person is turning inward, the process of empathy is a communication with the self. It is an intimate experience with the voice of interiority too easily ignored in the reception in everyday life. It is a process of internal journey that is not just an exercise of self-discovery but learning to have a kind relationship with oneself. Self-reflection empathy is concerned with awareness of the plethora of emotions that make our inner world fabric and accepting them without judgment, knowing where they are coming to their existence and their effects.

Self-reflection also encourages us to determine what we say to ourselves-
-the stories we produce about ourselves as individuals as well as our value,
ability, and potential. These stories are usually tinted with self-criticism and
suspicion, which reflect the spirit of unsuccessful experiences or a sense of
inability. It is at this point that empathy comes in transformative – in a way
in which we confront these stories lovingly, without judgment. As we talk to
ourselves with compassion, we start repatterning these stories, swapping
words of judgment with words of support and words of suspicion with
words of confidence.

Compassion in self-reflection involves amicably facing our weaknesses
and fears. It is a matter of being with the discomfort and letting ourselves feel
without the need to fix or run away at the same time. It is an element of
resilience because we gain an understanding that our battles and losses do not
diminish our value. Rather, they turn into a source of development and self-
awareness.

Additionally, insight enriched with empathetic caring assists us in
determining biases and blind spots that tend to affect our enabling capacities
to interrelate with other individuals. Through this recognition of inner
obstacles, we shall be able to comprehend their effects on our interactions
and relationships. This is a realization of the need to eliminate these walls and
be more truthful and understanding of the people that surround us.

Empathy as self-reflection is also the practice of setting the intention of
the way we want to be with the world. Learning more about the way we feel
and react to things can help us see things from the right perspective and
regard them with considerably more empathy. Such willed action not only
improves our well-being but also improves our relationships as we become
more sensitive to the needs and emotions of others.

The inclusion of empathy in personal contemplation is constituted by frequent actions, including journaling, mindfulness, or pausing and breathing. These habits open up room for self-reflection and enable us to go out there deep into our feelings and connect with them in a valuable manner. These reflective practices develop a more intimate relationship with the self, hence developing an ability to empathize better with others.

It comes down, after all, to empathy with oneself. It recognizes the fact that we are all a work in progress, and it is merely ourselves that requires some form of empathy and compassion when we are willing to show it to others. With such an attitude, we set ourselves on the path towards more understanding and deep-rooted relationships not only with the world but also with ourselves. That is how self-reflection would not be merely an individual activity but a primary way of habitually living a life that can be full of empathy and understanding.

EMPATHY AS A LIFELONG JOURNEY

Empathy is not articulated in the fabric of life as a limited technique that should be developed and learned but as a process that is ever-changing and that exists alongside people through the various paths of life. This view encourages a significant change in the way of thinking because empathy has ceased to be viewed as a goal and a journey of self-improvement and adjustment. Every experience and moment of life comes with its possibilities of enhancing and improving emotional and empathetic skills. This is an ever-evolving process that is neither time- nor circumstance-restricted, yet is defined by the determination to get to know, understand, and relate with others more profoundly.

The empathic experience starts with childhood, and building the experience in childhood invokes emotional intelligence in the future.

Children formulate and internalize lessons on empathetic attitudes by watching the pro-social behavior of the adults in their midst. These initial interactions are what foundational skills of empathetic response are based on as they develop. With the multitude of social struggles and experimentations of identity that are part of adolescence, empathy has a good environment to thrive. Kids at these early ages might have a lot to do with comprehending different minds and sentiments, and that can highly advance their empathy in case they are handled and taken care of in the right way.

Empathy automatization takes on different proportions as adulthood calls. Empathy proves to be a very useful tool to use in personal relationships to promote intimacy and healing of relationships. The skill to truly empathize and connect with the feelings of the other person can change relationships and can swing a possible conflict into the chance to become closer. Empathy has become one of the most important elements of teamwork and leadership in the professional environment. Leaders who develop an empathetic style have improved chances of instilling trust in employees, inspiring their teams, and negotiating through the dynamics of workplace relationships. This does not only improve culture in organizations but also spurs innovation and productivity.

During life, empathy is tested, and more experiences enhance it, such as cultural interaction and traveling/contact with other norms of living. These experiences open minds to defy preconceptions and increase the ability to understand nature with diverse people. These days of growing globalization and interconnection, bridging the gap between different cultural experiences with the help of empathy is more important than ever.

Empathy also transforms in the second part of life in a more retrospective form. Experience brings wisdom, and the older age one is, the more grayscale he/ she can perceive human emotions and motivations. Senior adults who have progressed throughout a variety of life experiences contain an immense sense of empathetic ability that can be used as a provision of light to younger generations. This reciprocal flow of empathetic wisdom gives further validity to the idea that empathetic wisdom is a lifelong pursuit, that it is something that enhances the person and the community.

Finally, the need to learn empathy as a lifelong process involves the willingness to learn new things and experience changes. It requires one to show eagerness to interact with the world and its people in a questioning and caring manner. Working on this quality in each corner of our existence, people will improve not only their emotional state but will also make our world kinder and more understanding. Through it, empathy is not only a journey of a person, but it is a topic of a community that can promise to bring a more interconnected and understanding world.

CHAPTER 10

Empathy in Communication

ACTIVE LISTENING

Active listening comes down to the idea that simple conversations are turned into a significant connection. It does not mean listening to phrases; rather, it means interacting with the speaker at a higher level, so he or she would feel that somebody cares or rather someone cares to get to know. This method needs the listeners to be in full focus and free of distractions and prejudices, which creates an ambiance conducive to the sense of authenticity in communication.

Fundamentally, active listening entails being mindful and placing the other in a position to speak with the awareness that the speaker will be listened to without any interruptions or judgment. This implies the ability to manage comfortable eye contact, make nonverbal signs, e.g., nodding, and use minimal encouragers, e.g., saying mmm or I see to indicate attention. It is an art of gracefully trying to balance silence with encouraging gestures so that the speaker will feel free to talk to his or her fullest without the fear of being interrupted or misinterpreted in the middle of the conversation.

Another important element is reflection and validation of what the speaker says. Instead of rushing to conclude and constructing a reaction, the listener mirrors what they heard. This may be phrased in the following way, "It appears that you are... or What I hear is... These reflections not only sound the truth but also help the speaker explore his or her thoughts and feelings further, thus making him or her speak more and creating a more elaborate discussion.

Issues like listening to respond to things instead of listening to understand are also some of the dangers that active listening helps to avoid. This will entail avoidance of the strong inclination to give personal responses in the form of examples or solutions to the story where it is not expected. As an example, when a parent is listening to someone recount a problem and describe the issue, there is always the temptation to tell the parent how one did it, but they really need to allow the child to tell his side of the story.

Some of the aspects that one can do to develop these skills include taking part in a role-play situation where they practice and learn dialogues that can be used in their profession and at personal levels as well. It can be a manager hearing what an employee has to say about a deadline of a project and being able to be empathetic and active in listening or a partner trying to be empathetic and listen to his/her loved one after a hard day; these exercises can teach those who are interested how to make such action effective.

Active listening also depends on the art of checking in regularly. Such minimal, considerate things as a short text or a verbal check-in can strengthen a bond and demonstrate that the other person is an important focus. This integrity brings trust, and later on, getting into serious discussions with each other becomes easy.

Besides, it is important to identify when and how often these check-ins take place. The proper time to call someone is when there is a hard time after a difficult meeting or when one is visibly distressed; this is because the offer will be very good and effective.

Listening, therefore, requires some active process with a person in the front rather than passive. It involves the establishment of a secure dialogue environment and the inclusion of both sides in which the partners feel honored and understood. This habit does not only improve individual relationships but also business relationships, and this makes the world empathetic and more understanding.

Non-Verbal Empathy

In human relations, a lot of what is being conveyed is conveyed without even talking. This non-verbal communication, usually even deeper than words, creates a power of non-verbal empathy. Non-verbal communication sometimes fills the gaps left by words, and the subtle look of the eye, the movement of the body, and the changing of the face are sublime messages of understanding and compassion. These essential non-verbal communication signals are the hidden currents of our conversations in muted existence, reciprocating the facts of human relationships and feelings.

Think of a scene when two people are in a state of bereavement. One thing word could not always effectively portray in this environment of high emotion is how to express support and solidarity adequately, but to sit, give a simple nod, or look with a warm, understanding glance can speak volumes. It is all about non-verbal empathy, where behaviors, instead of verbal communication, are the language of communication.

Non-verbal empathy is seen as having originated in our biology, and the mirror neurons phenomenon plays a critical part. To enable that, these neurons can be called empathy neurons; however, they enable us to feel in common by bringing the emotion of a person and making it internal to us. When we see a person suffering, our mirror neurons allow us to feel their suffering essentially on a gut level. This biological basis is what makes non-verbal communication very important in the development of empathy.

This effect of non-verbal empathy not only follows in an individual relationship but also reaches into the working relationship. Examples may include how a leader can pick up on the non-verbal aspects of his or her team to increase morale and develop team spirit in workplaces. A little thing like a pat on the back or a good job sign can reward the employee and also make him/her feel like he/she fits in.

Beyond that, non-verbal empathy is important in scenarios when using verbal means of communication may hinder communication or be misconstrued. Non-verbal signs present a universal method of expressing empathy and understanding, especially in multicultural environments, where language differences might become an obstacle. A common smile or a polite bow may lead to bridging the gap of language, and guilt and respect can be constructed.

Non-verbal empathy is also powerful because it reduces tension and facilitates the de-escalation of conflict. When a conflict arises, it is always important to keep open body signals and an unrestricted position that may lead to positive talk that may resolve the issues. This is not just a way of showing empathy, but it helps others show the same kind of emotions towards others.

Non-verbal empathizing needs wordlessness and deliberation. It is a process of being there and observing details of human behavior, including the minute ways people sit or change their facial expressions. Our improved sensitivity can increase our sensitivity to these cues, which helps us know even more about the emotional landscape of other people around us and engage in richer experiences among them.

Empathy, which is without words, empathy, which talks to the heart, is also an art. It is beyond the boundaries of communication, and it can give us a deep sense of communicating with others emotionally. In a world where we tend to use mainly words, it is striking that harnessing the force of non-literal empathy can change all our interactions, make our relationships even more complete, and make us know each other better.

Empathy in Digital Communication

The code of empathy becomes more prominent in the sphere of digital communication because there are no non-verbal elements such as those that characterize up-to-date gatherings between people. The digital environment, full of texts, emails, and chats, has sometimes removed such vocal tone, facial expression, and body language, which play a crucial role in sending emotional nuances. This loss may cause a lot of misunderstandings as the tone of the given message may be lost or misinterpreted, which would not have happened in a real-life situation of conversation.

The problem is finding a way to overcome this empathy gap so that our online words make enough impact and happen with the kind of emotional temperature that offline messages do. A typical trap in online messages is that it easily becomes possible to misinterpret them as cold or aggressive. A brief, to-the-point answer, although it is effective and effective, may be perceived as impolite or inconsiderate. To counter the latter, it may be helpful to introduce the aspects that encourage empathy, e.g., considerate punctuation, emojis, or deliberate verbal reassurance. For example, a small exclamation mark or a smile at the end of the message may change the overall impression and make it friendly and interesting.

Time and responsiveness are also important to the development of digital empathy. Later reactions may be construed as aloofness or indifference, even when it is not the intention. Thus, it can be sustained by having expectations about the response time and apologies for the delays. Even in situations when urgent answers are not possible, mere presence and support can be asserted through a simple text message like I am here in case you need me.

In addition, online communication offers a special condition of empathy that cannot always exist in real-life situations. The written form can have well-thought-out answers, and one can take time to come up with a supportive and understanding message. This is especially beneficial in tense or emotionally charged discussions, where a deft turn of phrase can diffuse a situation and provide evidence that the one speaking is sincerely caring and concerned.

Coming up with digital empathy also means taking into consideration the limits of the medium and making adjustments. This implies the apprehension that not every message should be answered swiftly, and there are times when it is enough to respond with a short note till there is time to come up with the most thoughtful response. One additional way to ensure a lack of misunderstanding and emotional connection is to encourage users to use voice memos or video calls in situations where the message is too complicated or in danger of being misinterpreted.

Digital empathy requires sensitivity and imagination. It gives us a hint to share some new means of showing care and understanding, like sharing a favorite meme or other emoji as a mood check or sticky notes with words of encouragement. These gestures may be simple, but they can communicate empathy in a way that words can't.

Finally, it is important to distinguish that digital communication demands an active manner of empathizing (it means that the emphasis is on establishing relationships that are not restricted by medium limitations). Through smart practices and the specific power of digital tools, we will be able to create fruitful interactions that are dense in empathy and insight, even at a distance. This method will not only overcome the implicit difference in digital communication but also turn it into a tool for constructive, more understanding bonds.

SCRIPTS FOR EMPATHETIC DIALOGUE

Writing empathetically means creating an atmosphere in which people build upon an atmosphere of understanding rather than judgment. Empathetic communication is not about the words to speak but rather the motivation that breaks a path toward connecting and respecting each other. Its essence is the idea of going beyond verbal exchanges and turning the process of dialog into a way of being together and a healing process.

Humane communication is in listening; this is an important part of empathetic dialogue. It means to go beyond hearing words and perceiving the feelings and intentions of the words. Active listening is a complete involvement through the mind to the speaker that actively manifests a listening attitude of understanding their emotions and perceptions. It is a matter of listening to the small signals of the tone of voice, the physical stance, and the unspoken, which many times drown speech itself.

It is critical to use the words when communicating in an empathetic way. One should use words that confirm and can identify with the other person as they relate their experiences and have concerns about them. Phrases such as I hear you, that sounds so difficult, or I can understand why you would feel that way are ways of confirming what the speaker is saying will diverse him. Such affirmations build a secure environment in which one feels acknowledged and noticed, which promotes trust and openness.

In addition, the empathetic conversation includes open-ended questions that prompt a person to think more deeply and speak. Questions like whether you can talk further about that! Or, as we say, what did that make you feel? Ask the speaker to linger more on their thinking and feelings. This would not only contribute towards getting a better idea about their point of view, but it will also show them that one is very much interested in what they are going through.

Empathetic dialogue also entails the ability to mirror whereby what a speaker tells is repeated in order to show comprehension and confirmation. This may be realized by paraphrasing or summarizing what the speaker has said so that he or she may feel appreciated and encouraged. It is a method that supports the rhetorical presentation made by the speaker and displays that what they said has been heard and acknowledged.

Silence is sometimes louder than words when it comes to empathetic conversations. Using silence to take pauses between communication offers the speaker a chance to think and rationalize feelings, which builds up the level of communication. Presence and patience may also be presented by silence, as this shows that the listener is attentive and encourages the person speaking.

Having an empathetic conversation is not all rosy. It needs patience, modesty, and the eagerness to shelve one's own biases and assumptions. It is the state of being in the here and now, with someone that is in front of you with no need to be hijacked by the thought of the person in front of you or even the impulse to reply and share the solution or give advice.

Eventually, the outcome of the empathetic conversation is to establish bridges of understanding and sympathy. It is about establishing an environment where people will feel enabled to share their realities with a minimum chance of judgment or disapproval. Via empathetic communication, relationships are stabilized, conflicts are overcome, and a stronger sense of community and connection is built. It is a habit that, when applied, can change not only personal but also the whole picture of human relations.

CHAPTER 11

Empathy and Creativity

EMPATHY IN ART AND LITERATURE

Empathy as a phenomenon is revealed in the world of art and literature as a strong bond between a creator and his audience that helps fill the gap between two different human experiences. With vivid colors that a painter puts on canvas or with well-structured sentences, the writer of a novel, empathy turns into a map through which the nuances of human nature are revealed and discussed.

With its many forms, art is a universal language that has no boundaries in terms of culture and words. It calls an audience to put themselves into the place of another person, to have access to other worlds and feelings that the audience never experienced themselves. As an example, consider a painting of a broken land in the wake of war; it is not only a depiction of a destroyed place, but it is also a plea to induce the viewer into empathizing with the sorrow, fear, and hardiness of all combatants. This is observant involvement, which is not confined to the arts of the eye. Music, with its capacity to express emotion by means of melody and rhythm, can result in profound emotional reactions, enabling the listeners to share the experiences of other people on a subconscious level.

Another strong source of empathy is literature, which has a colorful carpet of stories and characters. With the help of a narrative, people look through the lives of others with their problems and success stories. Readers can enter the minds of the characters of the novel written well because of the small details, and it corresponds to the feelings and motives even when those characters are living in a world that can be completely different from those of the readers. This literary sympathy is not only the understanding of the others but also of the humanity we have. It pushes readers towards addressing their prejudices and preconceptions and creates a more inclusive and emphatic perspective of the world in which they live.

Please think of the literature of the writers who portrayed the art of empathy in their narration perfectly. Their stories usually touch on the depths of human relationships and cover the issues concerning love, loss, and redemption. Their narratives are moving in that the tales reflect the twists and turns of real life, and eventually, the reader needs to introspect themselves and make them think about how they are behaving/treating other people.

The empathy in the literature is not subject to the word. It goes into the theater where actors play the role of people and recreate stories on a stage. This in-person performance is an active field of empathy because people see the development of the human drama live, experiencing the toll of raw emotions told by the performers. This closeness provided by the immediacy of theater encourages a special relationship between the viewers and the actors of the play, as they share the event of seeing a narration; they empathize with each other.

Besides, empathy in art and literature acts as a trigger to social change. Calling attention to injustices and underscoring the voices of the marginalized, artists and writers can engage in raising empathy-based action. They break the conventional rules and even ask questions that make people rethink their places in our world and their duty towards each other.

Empathy in literature and art is an agent of change in a nutshell. It not only helps us know more about others, but, more importantly, it adds to our emotional spaces. Through art and literature, we are invited to grow in our capacity to empathize, to understand the world in a multiplicity of ways, and to share the universal fabric of humanity. Such compassionate experience eventually creates a stronger bond with the world and with each other, proving the eternal strength of art and literature in creating and enlightening the human spirit.

EMPATHY IN INNOVATION

Empathy seems to be a distorted ingredient in the world of innovations. It is the door and the gate between the mind of the creator and the recipient, and it is used to apply abstract notions to real manifestations in life that truly connect to us human beings. The empathic innovators do not only design for people but also design with people firmly connecting with their lives and experiences.

The starting point of empathy in innovation is the skill to listen and observe without having preconceived ideas. It implies putting yourself in the situation of other people to know their problems, their want, and their feelings. This is not only about yielding information or administration of surveys but requires becoming acquainted with the world of the user. By placing oneself in the setting where this audience operates, innovators can find answers that are not two-fold evident, thus coming up with solutions that not only work but are also touching.

Think about the design of something basic, such as kitchen appliances or even mobile applications. A caring approach to those designs would be not only the utilitarian side but also the feeling of the user in the way they interact with such products. It is a way that can result in innovations that make the work easy, the experiences pleasant, and the joy gained. An example of an empathetic designed kitchen tool can be taken into the world of people with arthritis as this process may require attention by making life easier in the kitchen.

The aspects of empathy also have a significant effect on teamwork. As team members learn to be empathetic, a culture of exposing ideas and doing individual and group criticism without the fear of judgment is created. In such an environment, creative risks and innovation are promoted, and the person feels empowered in what he or she does. This can be done by humanitarian leaders willing to listen to their crew, seeking the insights of people with different opinions, and creating an atmosphere of inclusivity in which everyone is being listened to.

The whole notion of empathy-driven innovation, in a wider sense of social problems, creates an effective instrument of social change. It enables innovators to consider resolving complex problems in the fields of healthcare, education, and sustainability through those solutions that will actually satisfy the communities. To take healthcare as an example of a softer innovation, empathetic innovation can mean developing patient-centered care systems and taking into account the emotional and psychological patient requirements rather than issues. The health of the communities might lead to healthier communities through such systems that can improve patient outcomes and satisfaction.

More so, empathy in innovation does not only involve the introduction of new products or services but also the improvisation of available products to suit them to the extent of satisfying the users. The iterative process of innovation may be guided by continuous feedback loops in which the users are motivated to share their experiences and suggestions. This constant exchange of ideas means that products advance in relation to user requirements and preferences, and thus, they become updated and effective as time goes by.

Finally, empathy in innovation is all about humanizing the creation process. It asks the innovators to think not only about the technicalities and the profit percentages but also about the human implications of their vested efforts. With a strong emphasis on empathy, innovators will be able to come up with meaningful and transformative solutions rather than only technically competent ones, leading humanity towards living in a world where technology would not be the master but rather the servant.

EMPATHY IN STORYTELLING

Created to enhance one undeniable truth rather than fiction, empathy has become a great instrument that helps fill in the gap between the tale and the appeal. The art of storytelling is founded on the cornerstone of empathy and goes beyond retelling one incident to make it a resourceful tool for human relationships and communication. It creates a patchwork of feelings, thoughts, and lives that not only require the audiences to listen but also to watch, experience, and view the world through the lens of other human beings.

The core of empathetic storytelling is being able to put oneself into the shoes of others, to see through their eyes, and to feel like they feel. What it means is that storytellers need to get a closer look into the lives of their characters and their emotions and find out about their motivation. This explains why storytellers are able to tell stories that connect personally with people and transport them to a commonplace of emotional belonging.

A story must include empathy; not only do the plot and the character need to be realistic, but there has to be an authentic connection established between the audience and the storyteller. This connection is also elaborated with the help of the narrative arches crafted thoughtfully to reflect the dynamics of the real world with all its uncertainties, conflicts, and victories. In this way, narrators are able to appeal to the emotions of the people to whom they are recounting their stories by trying to elicit some form of compassion in them so that they can review their lives and the lives of the people around them.

Furthermore, compassionate narration offers a voice to the underprivileged views. It acts as the channel to make such voices heard, comprehended, and appreciated. Sharing stories that portray a variety of experiences and opinions, the storytellers will be able to take down stereotypes, break down walls, and foster a better comprehension of other cultures, backgrounds, and identities. Not only does it make the story rich, but it also can produce changes in societal perceptions and lead to inclusivity.

The effect of empathy-based storytelling is not limited to individual relationships because it affects how the broader narrative plays out. Empathetic stories could bring change, change minds, and start movements. They are able to point out social injustices, lead people into discussion of hard issues, and provoke them into action. With empathetic narration, the audience does not merely sit down as if they are being told a story but becomes engaged in an empathetic discussion, which could cause something actionable to occur.

The importance of empathy in storytelling is further enhanced in the digital age when the process of sharing stories becomes as widespread and swift as possible. The reach of free online platforms gives storytellers a chance to connect to a diverse set of people all around the world. This is the potential that empathetic storytelling utilizes to create bridges to close the cultural and geographical distance, to nurture cross-cultural empathy and understanding, and thus build an empathetic cosmopolitan culture on the planet.

In the end, empathy in storytelling is not merely about making a good story but also about the ability to create a story or use the story as a means of connection, understanding, and change. It encourages the audiences to put themselves in the position of other people, to look at the world through the eyes of other people, and to come out with a better understanding of what it is like being a human being. By so doing, empathetic storytelling can change not only the content of the story it tells but also the world in which one exists.

EMPATHY AS INSPIRATION

During times of peace in life, empathy as a way of guidance becomes a powerful driving force to create links of more than just understanding. It is a kind leader who teaches people to make great revelations and find a better connection. This unseen thread makes people connect and enables them to look further into the depth of another's experience.

Empathy has its origin in intense understanding of the sentiments of others, a feeling in the gut about their life and disappointments. It is a subtle realization that every human being has his or her struggles and ambitions. Such acceptance fires an inner fire, leading to actions that are deep and considerate. Listening entails the ability of a person to become a mirror that will reflect the fears and hopes that other people cannot articulate.

The revolutionary nature of empathy is based on the fact that it is a power that inspires change and innovation. Those people who interact empathetically start interpreting the world through various lenses, and each lens is unique, hence providing a different perspective. Such expanded perspective stimulates creativity because empathy provides the imagination with fresh sources of energy that question its original ideas and create new ones. It drives innovation, breaks boundaries, and builds walls that initially appeared to be impossible to break through.

Empathy is also a crucial part of leadership as this evokes loyalty and teamwork. Employees whose leaders act as empathetic individuals produce an atmosphere of effective communication and a sense of appreciation and understanding among team members. This feeling of ownership instills team spirit and loyalty, which pushes teams to attain group objectives. Knowing the needs and motivations of other people, empathetic leaders are able to inspire their teams and create a new level; they are able to create a shared vision that is inclusive and dynamic.

Personal relationships: empathy inspires closeness and respect in personal relationships. It invokes them to put themselves in the shoes of other people to experience the burden of the road of a stranger. This sympathy creates forgiveness and empathy that bind them more than the connections that must reunite them. Empathy promotes patience and forgiveness, which can result in relationships that can survive even under the condition of a setback.

Furthermore, empathy is not a personal and professional phenomenon; it spreads into society as a whole. It is a source of social justice and equality; it motivates people to support those whose opinions are usually not heard.

Being compassionate drives an individual to make a better change to an inclusive society that is more loving, where its people embrace differences in a manner that dignifies and respects them all.

Empathy helps make people feel motivated to give back to their communities, and through this, an impact is made, which trickles down the events beyond their local areas. It promotes international citizenship when the welfare of others starts being a common concern.

But finally, empathy as inspiration is the process of change, personal, relational, and social. It asks a person to think not only of himself but also to relate to others in a humane aspect and to be kind and compassionate. The inspiration is here to stay; it is to replicate an inextinguishable source of continual incentive to transform the world where empathy could be the key to every communication. It is a heart walk, a walk that instills value in life and helps in a mission and mission sense feeling.

CHAPTER 12

Empathy and Well-being

EMPATHY AND MENTAL HEALTH

Empathy comes out as a deep strand in the complex, rich tapestry of human experience, twining links that are both subtle and strong. It makes sense for mental health and provides some help in knowing the emotional landscapes of human beings. In essence, empathetic people are able to think and feel the same as another on a whole other level because this kind of ability establishes a connection that can bridge the seemingly insurmountable distance in regard to mental health matters.

Empathy has many levels, and all of them play unique roles in mental well-being. Cognitive empathy means having an intellectual comprehension of the viewpoint that holds the other. It is a mental game of taking over someone, where an individual puts themselves in the shoes of the other. On the other hand, there is emotional empathy, which is the gut reaction, the commonality of emotion, a thing that can be enlightening as much as it is burdensome. Compassionate empathy merges these components and causes an individual to act in order to take away another person who is in distress. These elements of understanding, connection, and support make up a full picture of how to take care of mental well-being as these aspects of empathy come together to make a cohesive whole in terms of mental well-being.

Mental health is especially important in the context of the relationship between empathy and therapeutic situations. Counselors and therapists cultivate empathy so that they can produce safe environments where people can discover that they are being listened to and understood. This understanding tact helps to build a trusting relationship, which is paramount in successful therapy, especially for a client who is allowed to touch on the mental topography without being judged. In addition, the understanding of empathy during therapy helps to recognize the specifics of mental health disorders and offer specific solutions to each person.

Besides the clinical setting, empathy is one of the main building blocks of daily interactions that impact mental well-being on a bigger scale. Empathy builds a protective wall against the isolation many individuals experience whenever having mental health issues. It creates a feeling of belongingness and understanding, which are important aspects of a positive social network. To those who have to cope with their mental health conditions, the kind presence of friends and relatives can offer peace and support that can counteract a sense of isolation and hopelessness.

Nonetheless, the connection between empathy and mental health does not stay that straightforward. When unchecked, empathy may result in emotional burnout or exhaustion, especially among caregivers and mental health workers. Discussed as such as compassion fatigue, this phenomenon clarifies the essence of setting limits and maintaining self-care. The most important part is to find a balance between being empathetic and self-preservation to maintain one mental health so that one can help others.

Empathy can also be a revolutionary element in the realm of mental health awareness education. Schools and institutions that focus on empathy in the learning programs encourage an atmosphere that appreciates emotional intelligence along with academic success. Not only will this strategy help students appreciate mental health more, but it will also prepare them to help others, promoting a culture of compassion and strength.

The importance of empathy in mental health covers even society, which contributes to the perceptions and policies of the population. The promotion of mental health also rests on empathy, which encourages the communities to look into the colors of mental health from a more caring perspective. This thinking fosters the movement toward dealing with stigma, facilitating conversations, and providing mental health support.

In effect, empathy is, therefore, an instrument and a panacea when it comes to mental health. Its power to link, heal, and empower people makes it very important in promoting mental health. With the help of empathy, it is possible to build environments in which mental health is not only recognized but welcomed, which opens the doors to healthier and more engaged societies.

EMPATHY IN STRESS MANAGEMENT

Amidst the fast life, stress has turned out to be a companion almost everywhere. But, buried deep in the crevices of our challenges in life, we can find the immense asset that can alter the face of the daily strikes of stress and empathy. This is usually an underestimated tool because it has been seen as the bridge between learning about our stress reactions and learning about other people; it creates a supportive situation, which tends to lessen the negative impacts of stress.

Empathy is actually the sensitivity to the feelings and emotions of others. It involves people getting out of their own experiences and seeing things in the eyes of a different individual. Empathy in stress management practice allows not only the individual to be self-aware of stress-inducing events but also to be sensitive and aware of stressors in others. This familiarity with each other constitutes an encouraging network, which is necessary for relieving and alleviating stress.

Practicing empathy enables humans to provide an arena of freely receptive communication in which they can express their stress without any reference to judgment and misinterpretation. This level of openness is very important since stress is usually amplified when a person is lonely or when other people cannot understand him or her. Empathy will reduce the intensity of stress by creating an atmosphere in which stress is discussed and can be jointly solved.

Besides, empathy promotes active listening, which is part and parcel of stress management. In empathetic listening, the listener is where the speaker is by giving him or her the full attention. Such listening is not only a validation of the experience of the person speaking, but it is a satisfaction or feeling to the speaker of being listened to and understood. This validation is an effective remedy for dealing with stress since people feel that they are not lonely.

Besides interpersonal, the fourth possible role of empathy in stress management concerns personal stress management. Through self-empathy, one will learn to approach treating oneself with the same care and compassion that an individual may have towards others. This is taking the time to be aware of the stress messages and being able to deal with them kindly instead of in a judgmental manner. Self-empathy enables a person to pardon themselves of shortcomings they feel they have, thus releasing the inner burden that, in most cases, aggravates stress.

Moreover, empathy is able to change the manner in which we view stress in itself. The empathy approach is able to reframe stress, taking them out of the burden-on-one perspective and putting them into a more general humanistic picture of being human. The perspective change reduces the weight of emotions and promotes the idea of joint efforts in dealing with stress. In collaboration, individuals can formulate techniques to manage widely experienced stressors, like management of workload or emotional support, hence reinforcing resilience and lowering the levels of total stress.

Emphasis can contribute greatly to stress management activities in a professional environment. When leaders use empathetic strategies, employees also find places of work to be accommodative and of value. Besides boosting morale, this boosts productivity as employees find it easy and more likely to contribute and work better in a caring environment. Leadership powered by empathy helps to create a culture of mutual understanding and respect, as stress will not be overlooked or stigmatized but will be accepted constructively and positively.

To sum up, empathy can also play a crucial role in stress management. Emotional alignment helps to relieve personal pressures and build the overall resilience of the communities, as having a wider perspective helps avoid hopelessness and emotional detachment. Amid the intricacies of contemporary life and management of the associated stresses, we can create healthier, more supportive and supportive cultures when empathy is embraced in managing everyday stresses.

EMPATHY IN PHYSICAL HEALTH

Empathy is considerably more proactive in the domain of physical health than the classical limits of medical care. The power of empathy in the healthcare environment is nothing short of being life-changing because it not only leads to the betterment of patient outcomes but also to the general experience of both the practitioner and patient. Once healthcare professionals interact with patients in an empathetic manner, they can fuse clinical care with an emotional support dimension, which enables the natural bloom of healing.

A doctor is going through numerous procedures in a hospital with a sterile touch, and fear of the unknown builds up. The role of the healthcare team cannot be overstated here: an empathetic attitude can change this experience. Healthcare providers will be able to produce a feeling of safety and trust by recognizing the emotions and concerns of the patient. This caring relationship will usually start with small efforts; deeper listening, eye contact, and nonverbal understanding can help serve as initial steps in this type of interaction.

Caring for physical health does not concern only emotional assistance but also has a practical impact on treatment outcomes. Research has indicated that patients tend to follow treatment plans faster in case administering health services personnel have shown compassion, making the patient spend fewer days in hospitals. The reason behind this is that more patients will open up about their symptoms and concerns and communicate freely with their patients when they feel understood and supported by them. Thus, the diagnosis will be more accurate, and their care plan will be more individualized.

In addition, empathy is very important in pain management. Pain perception is not just a physical experience, but it is also closely connected to emotion and psychological conditions. By recognizing and validating a patient in pain, the healthcare provider can actually change how the patient perceives his or her pain. With empathetic communication, a person is likely to turn on natural alleviating pain processes of the body, decreasing the use of medication, and improving health conditions.

Empathy also creates a partnering relationship between patients and care providers. Patients are also more likely to participate in the management of their conditions when they feel heard and listened to by the care providers. This teamwork is paramount in the treatment of chronic symptoms, where the patient should be involved in the use of long-term treatment regimens. The development of a relationship founded on empathy will result in the motivation of patients to be active during the health journey, which will help in the effective management of chronic diseases.

Moreover, empathy in medical practice is positive not only for the patient but also for the provider. Healthcare professionals may also feel better about working because burnout can also be reduced through the process of empathy. When service providers reach out to their patients on a humanistic level, it may also serve as a reminder of the actual gist of the job and will tap into the desire to do the job and give their all to their patients.

Empathy in physical health is a forceful and multi-dimensional instrument that alters the experiences of healthcare. It helps in communication, better treatment outcomes, and a healing environment beneficial to both the provider and the patient. Focusing on empathy will help healthcare systems approach a more holistic direction, in which physical well-being complements emotional and psychological one. This change towards a more empathetic treatment is not only a good decision out of caring but a smart one with its prospects that will lead us to the sphere where health care will be as much about healing the mind and soul as it is about treating the body.

EMPATHY AND HAPPINESS

Emotions are another chain of chain of human beings, and empathy becomes a power, tying the strands of joy and cognition. The relationship that exists between empathy and happiness is not coincidental by chance but exists deep in the context of human interaction. When people really empathize with each other, they appeal to a common fund of emotion that allows everybody to be joyful and content.

The idea of empathy, in its essence, implies the knowledge of and connection with what other people feel. This process of putting oneself in the situation of another person and seeing the world through his or her eyes is not only a social trait but also a way to discover emotional fulfillment. Whenever individuals are empathetic, they establish a bridge with emotions that enables them to connect with the experiences of other individuals so that their understanding of the human condition is more intricate and detailed.

Empathizing can result in great improvements in happiness. When people are empathetically active, they will have this feeling of belonging and a sense of purpose in life, which also adds to their wellness. This relationship rests on the fact that when people understand and help others, then they find meaning and fulfillment in their engagements. Empathy helps humans build strong and meaningful relationships, which is one of the pillars of happiness.

Besides, empathy cultivates community and sense of belonging, which are part and parcel of happiness. When individuals know that they can be understood and supported by other people, there is a higher possibility of them feeling secure and contented. This feeling of belonging is very important in a world of disconnection and isolation, and it can easily become the cause of unhappiness and despondency. Through establishing emotional bonds with others, one can fight these bad feelings and transform into a better and happier life.

Empathy also helps to minimize negative feelings like anger, frustration, and even loneliness. Empathy helps one neutralize any explosive situation and will create an atmosphere of tranquility and harmony. This skill of effortlessly flowing through the intricate landscape of emotions with ease and empathy can go a long way toward making people and a community happier.

Moreover, it (empathy) cultivates altruism, which has proven to make people happier and more contented with their lives. People usually find a great deal of happiness and satisfaction when they operate on behalf of others. This is good because this altruism, which is motivated by empathy, forms a positive feedback loop in that making others happy increases individual happiness, further encouraging further altruistic actions.

On the collective societal plane, it can cause very peaceful, collaborative societies all through empathy. Empathy being exercised in a group helps traverse a cultural and social gap, which creates an encouraging atmosphere where diversity is embraced, and mutual respect is the order of the day. Such a shared empathy does not only add to individual happiness but also the well-being of society as a whole.

To summarize, empathy is at the center of happiness and is closely connected to human experience. Empathy makes personal relationships better and increases the well-being of the community, as well as individual joy. Among many things that separate people or even build unwarranted barriers in our world of today, empathy is a beaming light of hope, leading people towards a better, harmonious, and complete life.

CHAPTER 13

❊

Empathy and Technology

EMPATHY IN AI AND ROBOTICS

Empathy is becoming a key factor in the fast-developing sphere of artificial intelligence and robots. With machines constantly taking a more prominent role in our everyday lives, developed skills and capacities to understand and communicate with people on an emotional level are becoming an issue of concern. This complex of technology and empathy has opportunities as well as challenges as it transforms the way we view interactions with machines.

The main focus of incorporating empathy in AI and robots is the creation of machines capable of imitating humanity's emotional behavior. These systems are also trained to read and guess human feelings using other factors like facial expression, voice tone, and body movements. In this way, because of analyzing this data, AI may react in a way that will seem to be thoughtful and attentive, increasing user satisfaction and input. As an example, the customer service robots that would possess empathetic mechanisms would be more able to handle stressful situations because they can react with proper emotional responses, which will enhance the quality of how people receive services and faith in them.

Besides, empathetic AI can find other uses other than customer service. In the medical field, empathetic robots may help in patient care by relieving them of the stress of day-to-day life, such as drugs, or by giving some moments of company to isolated patients. This may greatly improve the quality of care and the outcome of patients since all of them have physical and emotional requirements.

However, when it comes to the mission to cure AI with empathy, some ethical and technical concerns are being brought up. The greatest of these is making sure that people do not just end up with some systems that are capable of simulating empathy but not understanding or responding accordingly. This is a major ethical issue, as is the risk of creating machines that supposedly can generate emotions but do not understand them at all. This is compounded by the possibility of empathetic AI being used in the wrong hands regarding surveillance and marketing because emotions are the ones that can be used.

Empathy is ostensibly induced in machines using complicated algorithms and enormous data sets to set up AI models. Such models should be able to learn and adapt to a variety of emotional circumstances, which cannot be done without constant updates and renovations. The point is that it is a question of compromise between the technical affordances and ethical obligations of privacy and consent so that the data that will be used to train these systems can be used responsibly.

Creating empathetic artificial intelligence also needs cross-disciplinary work, where lessons learned in psychology, neuroscience, and ethics, as well as computer science and engineering, are applied. Such a collaborative model is needed because only in this way can it be achieved that the integration of empathy in AI and robotics should not only correspond to technical requirements but also to the values and norms of society.

To sum up, the question of empathy will become an important factor along with the development of AI and robotics. With the solutions to the technical and ethical issues, the power of empathetic AI could be used to make actual improvements in human lives. This may create a future where interactions between human beings and machines will not only be effective but also emotionally fulfilling, creating an easier coexistence between humans and technology.

DIGITAL EMPATHY TOOLS

In our present globalized society, online spaces also form a crucial aspect of everyday life and offer both phenomena and opportunities to show empathy. Since more and more communication is conducted through screens and devices, it is important to know how to express empathy in the digital realm. What differentiates empathy in digital communication is the essence of filling the gap, which arises in terms of emotion attached to textual communication. The main reason behind this gap is the lack of non-verbal signals, such as facial expressions and intonation, which are important elements of face-to-face empathy.

In order to cope with these obstacles, it is necessary to use digital empathy tools efficiently. As a communication aid, these tools are developed to help communication on an emotional level be clearer and definite. The use of emojis and punctuation to express tone is one of the most widespread ones. As an example, something as basic as a smiley face can help make an otherwise blunt message appear sociable. In contrast, the use of exclamation points helps make the message sound warm and enthusiastic. On the same note, a person can avoid misunderstanding by using carefully selected words and phrases that directly show a person that the other person is understood, such as placing a phrase after using words that clearly support the feelings that a person may be having. Such phrases can confirm emotions, as I know how you feel. That must not have been easy.

Scheduling is also another important pillar in digital empathy. Being a good listener and replying to messages quickly, especially when the messages cause some distress or need support, is also a sign of being empathetic. Nevertheless, it is also paramount to understand the boundaries of digital communication and when it is necessary to shift into a different type of interaction in which the more subtle means of communication are possible, including a phone conversation or video call.

The fact is that digital empathy deals not only with the content of the messages but also with the context of sending them. It is always good to learn the predicament that the other person may be going through, such as the current amount of work they have or their mood, etc.; this will enable the messages to be in line. To illustrate, a show of empathy and awareness can occur through an encouraging message prior to a large meeting or following a tough day.

In addition, digital empathy implies taking care of how often one communicates. Excessive messaging is seen as intrusive, and the insufficient amount of communication may be seen as neglect. A balance is healthy in that the recipient does not feel suffocated.

In digital communication, empathy also reaches the stage of checking in with people in creative ways. It can consist of sending a related article, a funny meme, or a kind video that touches on the interests of the second person or his personal experiences. These can show that you are concerned about them and you are cognizant of their welfare.

This means that as digital communication develops, our approaches to expressing empathy should alter as well. These digital empathy tools enable us to stay in touch with our lives and even enhance relationships with others, in spite of the spatial separations which, all too frequently, are imposed by the medium of technology. Learning how to deal with these tools not only makes the relationships with others more pleasant in everyday life but also in the workplace, as digital environments become less sterile and emotionless.

EMPATHY IN VIRTUAL REALITY

Virtual reality opens a new terrain of empathy where the distinctions between the user and the experience are no more than a barrier to connecting to the emotions and the subjectivity that were otherwise impossible. Virtual reality (VR) allows a person to enter the world through the eyes of another; hence, the feeling of empathy is strengthened when the person actually feels what the person is facing.

VR gives people the power to experience worlds and scenarios in their real form, where the experience is both visceral and transformative. This experience can appeal to various senses in VR, which makes it produce stronger and more true-to-life emotional reactions than traditional media. Such sensory immersion allows for the experience of the details of another person's reality. It helps to fill in the gaps in understanding between them, which is hard to bridge by usual means.

VR is also being used to impart the values of empathy in learning institutions through its ability to show how other human being live their lives. As an example, students may gain the virtual experience of becoming a refugee and living in a world of challenges and feelings that accompany displacement and uncertainties. Such exposure not only increases the level of empathy but also fosters critical thinking and compassion, where senior school students reflect on the complicated happenings that affect the lives of others.

VR in healthcare is applied to train professionals and gives simulations of what the patient experiences. This will enable medical personnel to be in a better position to understand the emotional and physical situations of patients, hence resulting in sympathetic care. Through the virtual experience of the symptoms of a condition, healthcare professionals will have an insight into the patient's situation, bettering patient-provider communication and outcomes.

VR is also being used in the corporate world to develop empathy within teams. Through VR experience wherein participants deal with workplace dilemmas presented in the minds of coworkers, the employee gets a better notion of various roles and duties, which encourages a friendly and compassionate workplace. This may have the potential to result in better team relationships and a more encompassing working environment.

Besides, VR provides an exceptional way of solving social problems because people are able to interact with situations that point out imbalances and injustices in the system. As individuals experience the effects of discrimination or bias firsthand as VR immerses them in these scenarios, the conversations and actions will be triggered to induce social change. Such experiences may be decisive in changing attitudes and behavior to help promote empathy as a means to achieve social justice.

Nonetheless, the moral aspects of VR, as applied to empathy training, have to be taken into consideration. Exposure to extreme situations can also cause fatigue of the emotions instead of amplifying them, predisposing them to emotional saturation or apathy, which is also possible. Also, the realness of the experiences should be well crafted to make sure that the experiences are exemplary and appreciative of the realities they are trying to address.

In conclusion, it is necessary to mention that VR is a potent means of training empathy since it tries to recreate the experience on a scale that is incomparable to other methods. With the development of technology, the opportunity of VR to alter our perception and extend our connection to each other is still growing, and its new potential is rooted in empathy and the ability to teach students, cure patients, and change people in general. Creatively used, VR can be the agent by which humanity is able to reconnect more deeply and lead to a world more interested in communication and empathy.

ETHICS OF EMPATHY IN TECH

In the world of fast technological development, the necessity to implement empathy in the creation and implementation of new tools and systems becomes regarded as one of the fundamental ethical aspects. With technology finding its way into every single territory of human existence, including communication and healthcare, education, and entertainment, the moral implications of the technologies introduce the need to evaluate not only the functionality and the efficiency of the technologies but also their ability to foster understanding and connectedness between users.

The moral theory of empathy in technology starts with the design process. Developers are urged to consider a human approach whereby the needs and experiences of the end users are considered the most important ones. This can be done by interacting with the various user groups and learning their problems and views. In this way, technology may be developed not only as a framework for efficiency concerns but as the framework that encourages the improvement of human relations and communications. An empathy-based design promotes inclusion and hence includes everyone in the technologies that are useful and offer accessibility to different abilities, backgrounds, and cultures.

In addition, with regard to the ethical use of technology, constant thinking and response is necessary. There is a need to evaluate the effects of the technologies each time they are being used. These include the collection of feedback, understanding the usage patterns, and openness to the changes, which would improve empathetic interactions. As an example, on social media platforms, algorithms could be tuned to show more valuable visual information, creating positive engagement between people rather than being sensationalist or polarizing.

The second important area of empathy in tech is the role of technology companies to take care of the privacy of users and information. In this century, where data is essentially called the new oil, a company has to evade the narrow path between using data to innovate and guarding the privacy of a person. This requires explicit information behaviors and the provision of user's access to their data. When you start thinking about ethical companies in terms of technology, you look at the companies that highly value the user experience because the welfare of the user is their number one priority as opposed to profit.

The empathy factor is also incorporated in tech-related companies' workplaces. An emotional environment fosters teamwork, creativity, and worker satisfaction. The leaders of technology are challenged to drive information openness and foster a culture of empathy through mental wellness and the importance of divergent opinions. This kind of environment is not only good for employees but it is also felt in the products and services that the company is dealing with.

Finally, empathy in technology emphasizes education and training, which are taken into account in the ethical spheres of technology. As future technologists and leaders are being nurtured, learning institutions are strategic places to instill empathy in their course curriculum. Teaching empathy to our children as a major competency in tandem with highly technical competencies will produce a generation of innovators who are not only people able to develop complex technologies but also people who are working to use those technologies in a way that contributes to the greater good.

To sum up, the ethics of empathy in technology is a complex issue that needs the joint efforts of developers, companies, and educators. Through focusing on empathy, technology can become an excellent driver of social good, undergoing an opportunity to bridge the divide and make the world more connected and caring. The way that must be followed is to identify that each technological breakthrough can either cause division or a bridge, and it is our moral responsibility to make it a bridge.

CHAPTER 14

The Future of Empathy

TRENDS IN EMPATHY RESEARCH

The study of empathy has undergone a radical transformation in the past years, and it is now no longer confined to the traditional parameters. Instead, it has expanded to several different spheres of study. This development is characterized by the increasing popularity of a new attitude to evaluating empathy as not only an inborn feature but also as an art that can be learned and developed. In addition to studying the static aspects involving empathy, there is a rising concern among the researchers, driven by the ideology of empathy as dynamic and capable of development through deliberate initiatives and interventions.

A dramatic change in the study of empathy emphasizes empathy as a flexible and learnable skill and not as a trait. This view is corroborated by longitudinal and intervention-led research that proves that empathy can be developed through practice within a period. According to such studies, empathy is not the one-dimensional overnight quality that is dependent on the innate characteristics of an individual but the one which a range of approaches, such as role-play games and mindfulness programs, could condition. These results highlight the life-altering potential of empathy training, stating that people can build their empathetic abilities under a well-organized effort.

Concurrently, meta-analyses have indicated that there is no doubt that after direct training and practice, empathy levels have increased. Such studies summarize the findings of various investigations and provide substantial arguments confirming the idea that empathy can be improved. The consequences of such findings are enormous, especially within the context of the educational and professional spheres, where empathy is now perceived as an important element of effective communication and leadership.

Studies on empathy have also gone as far as neurobiology with orientations over mirror neurons, giving some explanations about how mirror neurons have done a job over empathetic behavior physiologically. This study has shed light on how human beings can intuitively share and comprehend the moods of other people and present a scientific explanation of the phenomenon of empathy. Through the neural correlates of empathy, scientists understand empathy better in the way it takes place in the brain, thus creating more avenues in which empathetic skills can be honed with the help of neurological information.

In addition, the use of sympathy research has expanded into other practical areas, whereby empathy training innovations exist to mainstream both empathy training in business settings and education. Such programs tend to emphasize the development of all types of empathy (cognitive, emotional, compassionate, etc.), each playing its unique role in interpersonal interactions. Cognitive empathy is a psychic awareness of another person, emotional empathy has to do with sympathy for the emotional condition of another person, and compassionate empathy is a mixture of both of these empathies and the goal of offering assistance. With the help of these types, people and organizations will be able to establish more empathetic and supportive environments.

Stories about empathy are also being reinvented as social justice and inclusivity are now plotted into the narrative of empathy. It is a practice that is progressively being understood as a complex that will help resolve this split and create understanding among various groups of people. As a way of dealing with implicit biases and fostering social cohesion, researchers publicize empathy as a strategy for building more open and inclusive societies. This method focuses on how allies should be empathetic when identifying or applying different visions and thus help change the rest of society.

Finally, the history of the study of empathy suggests the expansion of the current knowledge about its complexity and flexibility. In accepting the concept of empathy as an achievable skill, researchers and practitioners are opening the doors to applying the concept in many areas, including individual growth and social transformation in a global setting. With the development of knowledge of empathy still improving, it carries with it the potential of deepening the ties between human beings and creating a more empathetic world.

EMPATHY IN FUTURE GENERATIONS

The trait of empathy can also be perceived as an important thread in the tapestry of human evolution, which joins people, families, and civilizations on the path of human evolution. Looking ahead into the future, the concept of empathy as it relates to the way in which future generations of people will develop and turn out raises the interesting question of pondering. This inquiry examines not only the ways to raise empathy in the minds of children but also how it can change to cope with the demands of a more complicated surrounding world in the future.

The basis on which empathy will be embraced in future generations will start with the stories and narratives obtained in the families and communities. Since early childhood, the children will be impacted by the emotional input that they acquire within their environment. As an ancient tradition, storytelling is an effective means in this sense. It promotes the ability to think about a situation through the lens of another person and emotional insights that prompt children to engage in the shoes of characters and, as a consequence, the people around them. This will foster the feeling of compassion and understanding, which can blossom in adulthood.

Educational systems also play a key role in establishing empathy in children who are going to grow up. Through social and emotional learning in the curriculum, the schools would deliver to the children the ability to know and learn how to handle emotions, strive positively towards goals in life, and empathize with people. This will not only boost academic work but also enable students to develop interpersonal relationships with sensitivity and understanding.

Emotional understanding is an essential ingredient of the changing family structure, whereby generation gaps are important to bridge. With the rise of blended families and the multicultural background it brings, empathy towards the divergent point of view has recently become a necessity. A culture of empathy can be promoted by rituals commemorating diversity and promoting open dialogue. Through activities that encourage listening and sharing stories, families will be able to build an environment in which empathy will flourish.

Furthermore, the era of digital life raises some challenges as well as opportunities for empathy. Technology may make us less in touch, but it presents us with new opportunities to communicate and get to know people. To a new generation, the art of digital empathy will come to be not only a skill but a must. Educators and parents could further guide the youth in evolving this aptitude by guiding them through the ins and outs of online communication with a sense of understanding and decorum.

It is also necessary to remove the obstacles like prejudice and bias that lie on the way to the cultivation of empathy among the generations to come. Society can assist youngsters in avoiding stereotypes and promoting diversity by promoting critical thinking and being open-minded. Inclusivity and culturally exchange-based programs can contribute to this process greatly, providing people of the future generation with the instruments to be empathetic towards the largest variety of cultures and opinions at their disposal.

All in all, empathy has a long way to go, and it exists in purposeful development in diverse walks of life. Future generations will benefit from empathy and will approach a more globally connected world via the use of storytelling, education, family rituals, digital literacy, and cultural inclusion. With their growth and development, these young minds will also develop their understanding and ability to relate to their fellow men and women, and we can be sure that empathy will be an important attribute of human interaction.

EMPATHY AND GLOBAL CHALLENGES

Living in a world that is both more self-connected and paradoxically divided, the issue of empathy and its role in resolving global problems crops up into significance. The multiplicity and maze of global challenges, including climate change, social disparities, and more, require a sophisticated perception and a compassionate way of handling them that does not reduce national boundaries and cultural diversity.

Empathy is a channel that points to different points of view and helps to realize the feeling of common humanity, without which these titanic tasks are unlikely to be overcome. Through developing empathy, people and communities can be in a position to understand the complexity of interdependencies in the world so that they realize that what occurs in one corner of the world may have a direct impact on the rest of the world.

Climate change is one of the most urgent worldwide problems that needs to be solved through cooperation and caring about each other. It is vital to comprehend the causes and effects of groups of people who are disproportionately impacted by the neglect of the environment. Empathy gives us a way of discovering the immediacy of the crisis as seen by the vanguard of people on the ground- whether it is a farmer struggling with unpredictable weather patterns or a coastal village struggling with sea-level rise. With empathy, it becomes possible to mobilize action, promoting policy change and sustainable action that will take into account not only the needs of the most vulnerable groups but also the needs of the most vulnerable groups.

Similarly, empathy is essential in handling social inequalities that, in most instances, are perpetuated by deep-rooted prejudices and past sins. Employee empathy challenges community members to focus on social marginality groups, listen to their stories, and support the initiatives that seek to eradicate oppressive systems. With empathy at the focus of such conversations, we develop safe spaces of healing and reconciliation through which inclusive policies that will ensure equity and justice can emerge.

In addition, empathy is essential in an attempt to surmount the intrigues of cultural differences, which, more often than not, may bring about misunderstandings and disputes. The world has gone into the age of globalization, and cultures clash more often than not; empathy provides the means to bridge that gap of cross-cultural comprehension and collaboration. It promotes open-mindedness and curiosity, which enables one to be open-minded and learn new things. Instead of eliminating the distinctions, this cultural understanding concerns the hype over them, creating a united global society where the differences in culture are perceived as a strength and not an obstacle.

The age of digitalization and a high rate of change in technologies also introduce its special problems and liberations of empathy. Although technology at times causes some alienation and anonymity, it provides mediums to work on such empathy-based programs that bring individuals who are miles/kilometers apart. Internet campaigns, virtual reality, and social media are all valid tools to develop this empathy, educate people about world issues, and bring them to action.

Otherwise, in education, empathy should become part of the curriculum so that, hopefully, in the future, generations will be ready to look at the world's challenges with compassion and understanding. Empathy education teaches students to become critical of their presence in the world and how they can change people around them, and the creation of such global citizens is vital in the modern interdependent world.

After all, compassion is not merely an individual attribute but a social requirement. This is what we can use to construct stronger and fairer world communities. It is unprecedented times, and empathy can provide the way forward that is both effective and just as well as humane. The empathy effect, as such, is not restricted only to the individual level of interaction but has greater implications on policies and the direction the world as we aspire to build will take in with empathy as the new normal and the exception as the unacceptable.

CULTIVATING A WORLD OF EMPATHY

On the road of promoting the generation of the world that is enhanced with empathy, one will find oneself in the stretches of stories that comprise that blanket of people bound by a multitude of twine. These stories occur in households, offices, and public squares where unlikely connections are formed across uncrossable chasms. Suppose a book club has a viewpoint swap night, where members put their opinions aside to walk around in other people's shoes. These efforts break the ice and revitalize relationships, as is the case with the reuniting of siblings after years of feud based on political differences.

The foundation of such stories is the strength of the communal ritual that acts as the channel of trust and sense of community. This solidarity of group practices gives a valid sense of belonging and social empathy, and it accompanies a reduction in prejudice and an increase in cooperation. The mass experiences in such rituals as community book clubs or efforts in the neighborhood show the transformational ability of communal experiences. As an example, it can be a monthly initiative to bring the empathy book club where one group of facilitators host it on a monthly basis or organize neighborhood story swap nights, where one can tell and listen to shared stories and build an understanding of one another.

It is possible to initiate such empathy-driven group experiences with step-by-step guides, with templates of book clubs, discussion circles, and service projects. Those purposeful meetings do not involve sharing events but listening and reflecting as well. Employing empathy walks, during which a guided discussion with local leaders, the older generation, or new immigrants is carried out, also enhances the life of the community. However, difficulties, like group resistance or apathy, might emerge, and it will be necessary to use methods that would help retain engagement and work on power imbalances. Inclusivity and participation can be supported through sharing the leadership responsibilities or their participants through anonymous feedback surveys.

There are great success stories and emulating models that feature initiatives with quantifiable community impact. Imagine a block association that limits local conflicts by having frequent empathy circles or a school that started a buddy system that pairs up students of different backgrounds. These illustrations promote the practice of empathy in advocacy and activism because empathetic interactions create bridges and avoid burnout. Advocacy that is not inflicted on affected communities but advocacy that is with affected community's underlines collaboration and understanding.

Passionate yet detached empathy in advocacy does not ignore perspective, but instead, it educates how a person can be passionate about what he communicates without demonizing the other party. The necessary tools are scripts and strategies that leave conversations open, e.g., we can disagree, but I want to know what is important to you. We must use empathy to harness resilience and self-care within long-term advocacy, using rituals and reflective practices to maintain hope. The regular gratitude practices of small wins, as well as debrief circles after advocacy events, strengthen the spirit.

The interface of empathy into various spaces is not only able to accommodate neurodiversity, disability, and cultural differences across the world. When empathy practices are inclusive, they honor individual and community-specific needs so that there is accessibility and consent to all actions. Therefore, building a world of empathy is not simply a dream but actually a reality that would lead to a more together and united social world. With shared narratives, community rituals, and compassionate advocacy, the foundations of empathy sown today will deliver a more caring future to everyone.